# Heirs and Legatees
## *of*
## Harford County Maryland

## 1802-1846

*Henry C. Peden, Jr., M. A.*

HERITAGE BOOKS
2008

# HERITAGE BOOKS
*AN IMPRINT OF HERITAGE BOOKS, INC.*

## Books, CDs, and more—Worldwide

For our listing of thousands of titles see our website at
www.HeritageBooks.com

Published 2008 by
HERITAGE BOOKS, INC.
Publishing Division
100 Railroad Ave. #104
Westminster, Maryland 21157

Copyright © 1988, 1992 Henry C. Peden, Jr.

All rights reserved. No part of this book may be reproduced or transmitted in any form or by any means, electronic or mechanical, including photocopying, recording or by any information storage and retrieval system without written permission from the author, except for the inclusion of brief quotations in a review.

International Standard Book Numbers
Paperbound: 978-1-58549-118-6
Clothbound: 978-0-7884-7249-7

TABLE OF CONTENTS

Foreword.........................................iv

Copy of Benjamin Jones' Distribution, 1802......v

Heirs and Legatees of Harford County,
    Maryland, 1802-1846.....................1

Copy of John Hall's Distribution, 1802.........52

Surname Index..................................53

## FOREWORD

Estate distributions in Harford County, Maryland are contained in books as a separate record beginning in 1802. Prior thereto, there is a key or index to the administrations granted, inventories returned, and accounts passed by the Orphans' Court beginning in 1777. Prior to 1774, Harford County was part of Baltimore County. Had it not been for the fact that the Register of Wills and the Clerk of the Court were housed in a vaultlike wing of the courthouse, all of their records would have been lost in the fire of February 19, 1858. The main building was totally destroyed and with it the records of the County Commissioners and the earlier administrative bodies.

A distribution is a record that shows how the balances remaining in an estate after all claims have been satisfied are distributed among the heirs. On the following page, for example, is the distribution of Benjamin Jones, and on page 52 is that of John Hall, both of which are illustrative of the language common to estate distributions in 1802.

The information in this book was taken from "Estate Distribution Book No. 1, T.S.B., 1802-1845" in the Register of Wills Office in Bel Air, Maryland. The book actually contains estate distributions from March, 1802 through March, 1846. Information of importance to genealogical researchers has been abstracted, primarily the names of the deceased, the dates of distributions, the names of administrators, and the names of heirs and legatees. The information was compiled as shown in the record book. Spellings of names were also copied as they were written, even though obvious errors were found. For example, we find the name "Amos" and "Amoss" in the same distribution. And unless it was specified in the distribution, no relationship between family members was assumed by the compiler.

Estate distributions are important because there are times when not all of the heirs are mentioned by name in the deceased's will, or there might not have been a will. An example of the former situation is the will of Martin T. Gilbert in 1837. He mentions his sons by name, and not his daughters, but in the distribution of his estate later on, his daughters are named, but not his sons. The two records together give the names of all his children.

For saving time and space in this book, the following abbreviations are used:

        DOD -- Date of Distribution
        ADM -- Administrator/Administratrix
        ADN -- Administrator De Bonus Non
        H&L -- Heirs and Legatees

My special thanks to Harry L. W. Hopkins, Register of Wills, Maria Chumbler, Chief Deputy, and JoAnn Boyle, Deputy, for their aid and support while I worked on this project.

                                                  Henry C. Peden, Jr.

May 15, 1988

ESTATE DISTRIBUTION OF BENJAMIN JONES, HARFORD COUNTY, MARYLAND, 1802

Dr. Charles Jones Surveying Executor of Benjamin Jones late of Harford County Deceased

| Description | £ | s | d |
|---|---|---|---|
| To the Ballance of your final account passed on the 16th day of November 1802 and Recorded in the office of the Register of Wills amounting to --- | 90 | 4 | 6 |
| By Distribution as follows (to Wit) | | | |
| To Sarah Jones the widow of the Deceased one third part of the personal Estate as Directed by the deceased Will | 30 | 1 | 6 |
| To Sarah Wright one of the heirs as directed by the deceased Will one bow a legacy of the value of | 5 | " | " |
| To Frances Jones one of the heirs a legacy as directed by the Deceased Will one bow of the value of | 5 | " | " |
| To Rebecca Jones one of the heirs a legacy as directed by the Decd. Will one bow of the value of | 5 | " | " |
| To Stephen Jones one of the heirs as directed by the Deceased Will his Dividend of the personal Estate | 5 | 12 | 10½ |
| To Benjamin Jones one of the heirs as directed by the deceased Will his dividend of the personal estate | 5 | 12 | 10½ |
| To Charles Jones one of the heirs as directed by the Decd. Will his dividend of the persl. estate | 5 | 12 | 10½ |
| To Sarah Wright one of the heirs as directed by the Decd. Will her dividend of the personal estate | 5 | 12 | 10½ |
| To Rachel Jones one of the heirs as directed by the Deceased Will her dividend of the Personal Estate | 5 | 12 | 10½ |
| Amount carried over | 79 | 5 | 10½ |
| Amount brought forward | 79 | 5 | 10½ |
| To Elizabeth Brunley one of the heirs as Directed by the deceased Will her dividend of the personal Estate | 5 | 12 | 10½ |
| To Frances Jones one of the heirs as directed by the deceased Will her dividend of the personal Estate | 5 | 12 | 10½ |
| To Rachel Jones one of the heirs as directed by the Deceased Will her dividend of the personal Estate | 5 | 12 | 10½ |
| | 90 | 4 | 6 |

ex: by A.S. Test Abraham Jarrell R.W.H.C.

# HEIRS AND LEGATEES OF HARFORD COUNTY, MD, 1802-1846

**JOHN HALL OF CRAMBURY**
DOD: March 22, 1802    ADN: Josias Hall
H&L: Mrs. Hall, widow; John B. Hall; Edward Hall; Josias Hall; Avarilla Patterson; Priscilla Christie; Mary Hall; Elizabeth Hall.

**BENJAMIN JONES**
DOD: November 16, 1802    ADM: Charles Jones
H&L: Sarah Jones, widow; Sarah Wright; Frances Jones; Rebecca Jones; Stephen Jones; Benjamin Jones; Charles Jones; Rachel Jones; Elizabeth Brinley.

**BALCHER MICHAEL**
DOD: June 1, 1802    ADM: Ann Michael and Jacob Michael
H&L: Mrs. Michael, widow; John Michael; James Michael; Bennet Michael; Jacob Michael; Susannah Mitchell; Daniel Michael; William Michael; Josias Michael; George Michael; Martha Osborn; Aquila Michael; Elizabeth Michael; Henry Michael.

**CHARLES HUGHES**
DOD: June 1, 1802    ADM: Thomas Hope
H&L: Thomas Hughes; John Hughes; Timothy Hughes; Mary Hughes; Elizabeth Hughes; Sarah Hughes; Jane Hughes; Samuel Hughes; Joseph Hughes; George Hughes; Margaret Hughes; Ann Hughes; Susannah Hughes; Martha Hughes.

**WILLIAM MURPHY**
DOD: June, 1802    ADM: Ford Armstrong and Susannah Armstrong
H&L: Mrs. Murphy, widow; John Murphy; Frances Murphy.

**DANIEL ANDERSON**
DOD: June 9, 1802    ADM: Rachel Anderson and James Anderson
H&L: Rachel Anderson, widow; John Boman, husband of daughter of deceased; James Horner, husband of daughter of deceased; Charles Anderson; Mary Ford; and "8 other heirs" unnamed.

**LESTER ST. CLAIR**
DOD: August 10, 1802    ADM: Martha St. Clair
H&L: Martha St. Clair, widow; Hannah St. Clair; Mary St. Clair; William St. Clair; George St. Clair; James St. Clair; Amy St. Clair; Masannah St. Clair; Martha St. Clair; Elizabeth St. Clair; John St. Clair.

**LEVIN HILL HOPKINS**
DOD: August, 1802    ADN: John W. Hopkins
H&L: Frances Hopkins, widow; Elizabeth Hopkins; Joel Hopkins.

**EDWARD WARD**
DOD: August 17, 1802    ADM: Cassandra Ward and Richard Ward
H&L: Cassandra Ward, widow; Avis Kenly; Margaret Crawford; Mary Disney; Edward Ward.

JOHN DAY OF JNO.
   DOD: June 2, 1802          ADM: James Weatheral
   H&L: Sarah Day, widow; James Maxwell Day; Goldsmith Day;
        Elizabeth Maxwell Day; Mary Goldsmith Day; Martha
        Goldsmith Day; Frances Day; Rhoderick Day.

CASSANDRA SHEREDINE
   DOD: April 24, 1802        ADM: Daniel Sheridine
   H&L: Nathan Rigbie Sheridine

GEORGE DOUGHERTY
   DOD: February 9, 1802      ADM: Margaret Taylor (Dougherty)
   H&L: Margaret Taylor, formerly Dougherty, widow; John Dougherty;
        Mary Ann Dougherty.

JOHN DAY OF JNO.
   DOD: August 24, 1802    ADM and H&L: Same as June 2, 1802.

NATHAN RIGBIE
   DOD: August 25, 1802       ADM: Daniel Sheridine
   H&L: Nathan Rigbie Sheridine; Cassandra Johns, daughter of
        Hannah Johns; Sarah Johns, daughter of Hannah Johns;
        Polly Johns, daughter of Hannah Johns; Amy Johns, daughter
        of Hannah Johns; Caroline Johns, daughter of Hannah Johns.

JEREMIAH SHEREDINE
   DOD: April 5, 1802         ADN: Daniel Sheredine
   H&L: Nathan Rigbie Sheredine.

HUGH ELY
   DOD: August 24, 1802    ADM: Joseph Warner and Jacob Balderson
   H&L: Ruth Ely; William Ely; Mary Cooper; Rachel Ely.

JAMES CAIN
   DOD: September 7, 1802     ADM: Elizabeth Cain
   H&L: Elizabeth Cain, widow; John Cain; Mathew Cain; Nancy Cain;
        Mary Cain; Jane Cain.

HUGH ELY
   DOD: September 7, 1802  ADM and H&L: Same as August 24, 1802.

ENOCH SPENCER
   DOD: September 7, 1802     ADM: Mahlon Spencer
   H&L: Sarah Spencer, widow; Hannah Burnett; Ann Ely.

JOHN HUGHSTON
   DOD: September 7, 1802     ADN: John Dutton
   H&L: Thomas Wathom; Elizabeth Hughston.

WILLIAM BULL
   DOD: September 7, 1802     ADM: Sarah Bull
   H&L: Sarah Bull, widow; Walter Bull; Billingslea Bull;
        Elisha Bull; Sarah Bull; Rachel Bull.

CATHERINE ANDERSON
   DOD: September 21, 1802    ADM: Hugh Anderson
   H&L: Hugh Anderson; Mary Renshaw; Eleanor Clark; Elizabeth
        Anderson; Ann Anderson.

**WALTER PERDUE**
    DOD: October 12, 1802    ADM: Walter Perdue
    H&L: Mary Perdue, widow; Rachel James; Walter Perdue.

**SAMUEL WORTHINGTON**
    DOD: October 26, 1802    ADM: John Worthington
    H&L: Charles Lee, son of Josiah and Sarah Lee; Joseph Henly; Mary Litton; Soloman Rees; Christian McWilliams.

**JAMES MOORES**
    DOD: September 21, 1802    ADM: John Moores, Esq.
    H&L: Mrs. Moores, widow; Daniel Moores; John Moores, Esq.; Deliverance Howard; Sarah Briarly; James Moores; Elizabeth Glascow; James Glascow.

**JOHN PATTERSON**
    DOD: November 2, 1802    ADM: George and Averilla Patterson
    H&L: Averilla Patterson, widow; Mary Frances Patterson; Sarah Eliza Patterson.

**JAMES PRESTON**
    DOD: November 30, 1802    ADM: Mary Preston
    H&L: Mary Preston, widow; Rachel Preston; Gideon Vanclave Preston; Sarah Ruff Preston; James Barnard Preston.

**ANDREW LINDSEY**
    DOD: December 8, 1802    ADM: Elizabeth Lindsey
    H&L: Elizabeth Lindsey, widow; William Lindsey; Robert Lindsey; Jane McCausling; Andrew Lindsey; Elizabeth Lindsey.

**DAVID FORD**
    DOD: December 14, 1802    ADM: Abm. Cord
    H&L: Mary Ford, widow; Rebecca Ford; John Ford; Betsey Ford; Soloman Ford; Sarah Ford.

**HOLLIS HANSON**
    DOD: February 19, 1802
    ADM: William Wilson, of William, and John Monks.
    Distribution of negroes to Greenbury D. Hanson & Benedict Hanson.

**HENRY THOMAS, JR.**
    DOD: February 8, 1803    ADM: Betty Thomas and Ralph Pyle
    H&L: Betty Thomas, widow; David Thomas, brother of deceased; James Thomas, brother of deceased; Hannah Thomas; Sally Thomas; Henny Poteet, formerly Thomas.

**JAMES WARD**
    DOD: February 1, 1802    ADM: Thomas Mitchell
    H&L: Ann Ward, widow; Elizabeth Ward; William Ward; Ann Ward.

**DAVID CHELSON**
    DOD: February 15, 1803    ADN: Henry Murphey
    H&L: Mary Chelson, widow; John Chelson; Lethra Chelson; Walter Chelson; Sarah Chelson.

**BALTIS FYE**
    DOD: 1803    ADM: William Fowler
    H&L: Mary Fye, widow; Jacob Fie; Balis Fie; Mary Fie.

ABRAHAM TAYLOR
DOD: April 13, 1803  ADM: Joseph Ford
H&L: Isabel Taylor, widow; Aquila Taylor; George Taylor; Bennet Taylor.

JOHN DURHAM
DOD: April 14, 1803  ADN: Cassandra Durham
H&L: Elizabeth Durham, widow; Cynthia Hays; Elizabeth Hughs; Emelia Beans; Celia Durham; Susannah Hillen; Cassandra Durham.

WILLIAM EVOTT
DOD: April 12, 1803  ADM: Margaret Evott and William Beaty
H&L: Margaret Evott, widow; Isabel Wiley; Jane Wiley; John Evott, Sr.; John Evott, Jr.; William Evott, of Richard; Joseph McElrath, Jr.; Martha Glenn; Sarah Bonar, wife of William Bonar; William Beaty, of Archabald; Isabel Armstrong; James Sheridine, a bound boy.

EDWARD PERRY
DOD: May 3, 1803  ADM: John and Frances Sanders
H&L: Frances Sanders, wife of John Sanders, formerly Perry, widow of deceased; Alse Perry, now Stricklen; Martha Summers, formerly Perry; Hannah Perry; Peter Perry.

VINCENT RICHARDSON
DOD: April 26, 1803  ADM: Martha Richardson and John Norris
H&L: Martha Richardson, widow; Benjamin Richardson; Cintha Bond; Harriott Richardson.

THOMAS SMITH
DOD: May 4, 1803  ADM: John Criswell
H&L: Hannah Smith, widow; Ralph Smith; Hugh Smith; Thomas Smith; John Smith; Susannah Gorrell; Olevia Ingrim; Elizabeth Barrett; Mary McCracken; William Smith; Nathaniel Smith; James Smith.

THOMAS BROWN
DOD: May 9, 1803  ADM: Mary Brown, now Everist
H&L: Mary Everist, formerly Brown, widow; Jacob Brown; Polly Brown; Elizabeth Chauncey.

HENRY GREEN
DOD: April 12, 1803  ADM: Bennet Bussey and Henry Cooper
H&L: Ann Bussey; Mary Cooper; Elizabeth Green; Martha Green; Sarah Green; Susannah Green.

HENRY GREEN
DOD: May 10, 1803  ADM and H&L: Same as April 12, 1803.

MARY ANN DAY
DOD: June 28, 1803  ADM: Henry Wetherall
H&L: Henry Wetherall; William Wetherall; Ketty Wetherall; James Wetherall; Sarah Golsmith; Elizabeth Watters; Mary Brown.

NICHOLAS BAKER
DOD: March 2, 1802  ADM: Agnes Bonar, formerly Baker

NICHOLAS BAKER (continued)
    H&L: Agnes Boner, widow; Mary Mears; Nicholas Baker;
    Martha Presbury.

JOHN BAKER
    DOD: November 16, 1802    ADM: Cordelia Baker
    H&L: Cordelia Baker, widow; Charles Baker; Gideon Baker;
    William Baker; James Baker; Sarah Brown, formerly Baker;
    Rachel Smith, formerly Baker.

ZACHARIAH STROBLE
    DOD: August 10, 1803    ADM: Cassandra Stroble
    H&L: Cassandra Stroble, widow; Zachariah Stroble; William Stroble.

HUGH ELY
    DOD: August 10, 1803    ADM: Joseph Warner and Jacob Balderson
    Further dividends to Ruth Ely, Mary Cooper, and Rachel Ely.

SAMUEL GRIFFITH
    DOD: March 1, 1803    ADM: Elijah Davis and Francis Garrettson
    H&L: Martha Griffith, widow; Miss Frances Garrettson; Miss
    Frances Griffith; Miss Sally Griffith; Samuel G. Griffith;
    John Hall Griffith; Edward Griffith; Luke Griffith;
    Alexander Griffith; Martha Smith.

SAMUEL KIMBLE
    DOD: 1803    ADM: Sarah Kimble
    H&L: Sarah Kimble, widow; James Kimble; Rachel Taylor; Hannah
    Taylor; Bethia Ayres; Jemima Dorsey; Susanna Cowen;
    Zachariah Kimble; Elijah Kimble; Naoma Kimble; Semela
    Kimble.

SAMUEL GRIFFITH
    DOD: September 1, 1803    ADM and H&L: Same as March 1, 1803.

JOSEPH TOWNSLEY
    DOD: November 15, 1803    ADM: Margaret Martain (Townsley)
    H&L: Margaret Martain, formerly Townsley, widow of deceased;
    John Townsley; Joseph Townsley; William Townsley;
    James Townsley.

JOSEPH BROWNLEY
    DOD: January 10, 1804    ADM: Catherine Brownley
    H&L: Catherine Brownley, widow; Ann Brownley; Sarah Barron
    Brownley; Eleanor Brownley; Joseph Brownley; Thomas
    Brownley; Catharine Brownley; James Brownley; John
    Brownley.

JOHN STUMP, SR.
    DOD: February 15, 1804    ADM: John Stump
    H&L: John Stump; Herman Stump; Hannah Stump.

JOSEPH WILEY
    DOD: February 14, 1804    ADM: William Evott
    H&L: Alse Wiley, widow; John Wiley.

WILLIAM BROWNING
    DOD: March 27, 1804    ADM: Peregrine Browning
    H&L: Martha Browning.

**RICHARD BRYARLY**
DOD: March 27, 1804   ADM: Ann Smith, formerly Bryarly
H&L: Ann Smith, formerly Bryarly, widow; Robert Bryarly; Margaret Dods; Thomas Bryarly; Eby Corbet; George Bryarly; Betsy Logue; heirs of Rev. George Worsley, deceased; heirs of Henry Bryarly, deceased.

**ROBERT SMITH**
DOD: April 11, 1804   ADM: William Smith
H&L: Jane Smith, widow; Lyle Smith; Samuel Smith; Robert Smith; Elizabeth Linsley, wife of Andrew Lindsey; Sarah Rigdon, wife of Baker Rigdon; Jane Smith.

**JOHN BROWN**
DOD: August 24, 1803   ADM: Susanna Brown
H&L: Susannah Brown, widow (plus share of Mary Brown who died a minor); William Brown (plus share of Mary Brown who died a minor); Aquila Brown (plus share of Mary Brown who died a minor); Martha Brown.

**CHARITY T. WHEELER**
DOD: April 24, 1804   ADM: Benjamin Green
H&L: Thomas Wheeler, half-brother; Benjamin Wheeler, half-brother; Josias R. Wheeler, half-brother; Sally Lilly, half-sister, wife of Joseph Lilly; Nancy Thomas, half-sister, wife of Giles Thomas; Mary Boman, half-sister, wife of Robert Boman; Elizabeth Donagan, half-sister; Michael Wheeler, brother; Frances Hellen Wheeler, sister.

**BENJAMIN CROCKETT**
DOD: April 24, 1804   ADM: William McMath
H&L: Sarah McMath, wife of William McMath.

**ANN WHITEFORD**
DOD: April 11, 1804   ADM: Alexander Cooper
H&L: Anna Gibson, wife of Jacob Gibson; Anna Cooper, wife of Alexander Cooper; Anna Cooper, daughter of Mary Cooper; Anna Gibson, daughter of Anna Gibson; Jacob Gibson, son of Anna Gibson; Margaret Gibson, daughter of Anna Gibson; George Gibson, son of Anna Gibson; Mary Gibson, daughter of Anna Gibson; Thomas Gibson, son of Anna Gibson; Jane Gibson, daughter of Anna Gibson; Alcey Cooper, daughter of Mary Cooper; John Cooper, son of Mary Cooper; Mary Cooper, daughter of Mary Cooper; Matilda Cooper, daughter of Mary Cooper; Hugh Whiteford, son of deceased.

**NATHANIEL BAYLESS**
DOD: March 27, 1804   ADN: Thomas Jeffery and James Stephenson
H&L: Ann Whitaker, wife of Platt Whitaker; Samuel Bayless; Daniel Bayless; Elizabeth Kenly, wife of Lemuel Kenly; Benjamin Bayless; Mary Bayless; Harriott Bayless; James Bayless; Nathaniel Bayless.

**RICHARD BRYARLEY**
DOD: 1804   ADM: Ann Smith, formerly Bryarley
H&L: Ann Smith, widow; Robert Bryarley, brother; Margaret Dods, sister; Thomas Bryarley, brother; Eby Corbet, sister; George Bryarley, brother; Betsy Logue, sister; children of Ann Wesley, sister; heirs of Henry Bryarley, deceased, brother.

HENRY SCARFF, SR.
 DOD: August 22, 1804      ADM: Henry Scarff, Jr.
 H&L: Patty Scarff, widow; Elizabeth Scarff, daughter;
     Patty Games, daughter; Henry Scarff, son.

BENNET MATHEWS
 DOD: August 29, 1804      ADM: Roger Mathews
 H&L: Joseph Mathews; Carvel Mathews; Roger Mathews;
     Miss Fanny Mathews; Miss Neoma Mathews.

AMOS BARNES
 DOD: August 14, 1804      ADM: Bennet Barnes
 H&L: John Barnes, son; Sarah Barnes; daughter; Garrett
     Barnes, son.

JAMES DEBRULAR
 DOD: November 28, 1804   ADM: Micajah Debrular & John Roberts
 H&L: Micajah Debrular, son; Benjamin Debrular, son; Cordelia
     Debrular, daughter; and another child, unnamed.

ALEXANDER GARRETT
 DOD: December 11, 1804   ADM: Martha McKernan (Garrett)
 H&L: Martha McKernan, widow; Ann Garrett, daughter; Eleanor
     Garrett, daughter; Elizabeth Garrett, daughter; Rosanna
     Garrett, daughter; Mary Ann Garrett, daughter.

ROBERT DUTTON
 DOD: December 12, 1804   ADM: Mary Dutton and John Dutton
 H&L: Mary Dutton, widow; Susannah Norris, daughter; John
     Dutton, son; Elizabeth Dutton, daughter.

JOHN HUGHSTON
 DOD: August 11, 1803      ADN: John Dutton
 H&L: Thomas Waltham Hughston, son; Elizabeth Dutton, daughter.

MOSES PITCOCK
 DOD: May 14, 1805    ADM: Elizabeth and Jonathan Pitcock
 H&L: Elizabeth Pitcock, widow; Jonathan Pitcock; Sarah
     Pitcock; Eleanor Woodard; Benjamin Pitcock; Charles
     Pitcock; Hannah Pitcock.

ROBERT GLENN
 DOD: February 15, 1804      ADM: William Glenn
 H&L: Joshua Miles, who intermarried with Jane, one of the heirs;
     David Streett, who intermarried with Hannah, one of the heirs;
     Roger Street (Rogers Streett), who intermarried with Catharine,
     one of the heirs; Nicholas Gorsuch, who intermarried with
     Nancy, one of the heirs; William Glenn; Isabel Glenn, widow.

SAMUEL McMATH
 DOD: March 27, 1805      ADM: William McMath
 H&L: Mary McMath, widow; Mary McMath, daughter.

RACHEL ELY
 DOD: April 9, 1805      ADM: Ely Balderson
 H&L: Stephen Chapman, grandson; Nicholas Chapman, grandson;
     Rachel Ely, of Joseph, niece; Rachel Ely, of Mahlon, niece;
     Thomas Ely, brother; William Ely, brother; wife of Joseph
     Ely, brother; Martha Balderson, sister.

JOHN HUGHSTON
DOD: February 12, 1805    ADN and H&L: Same as August 11, 1803.

JONAS STEPHENSON
DOD: April 23, 1805    ADM: Elijah Kimble
H&L: Mary Stephenson, widow; Sarah Hughes, daughter; Avis Hughes, daughter; Cordelia Gorden, daughter; Averilla Gorden, granddaughter; Rebecca Kimble, granddaughter; Farmer Elisha Stephenson, son; Mary Frances Stephenson, daughter.

HENRY WARFIELD
DOD: June 18, 1805    ADN: Jonas Courtney
H&L: Jacob Warfield, son; Bazel H. Warfield, son; Henry Warfield, son; Caroline Osborn, granddaughter.

JOSEPH EVERIST
DOD: June 12, 1805    ADM: Joseph Everist
H&L: Joseph Everist, son; Eleanor Taylor, daughter; heirs of Elizabeth Greenfield, daughter; heirs of Mary Michael, daughter; Samuel Everist, son.

HERMAN STUMP
DOD: August 21, 1805    ADM: John Stump
H&L: Elizabeth Jarrett, formerly Stump, widow; Hannah Stump, daughter; Mary Stump, daughter; Ann Stump, daughter; William W. Stump, son.

SAMUEL WILSON
DOD: August 21, 1805    ADM: Mary Wilson and William Wilson
H&L: Mary Wilson, widow; Cassandra Wilson; Elizabeth Cox, formerly Wilson; Lee Wilson; Rachel Wilson; Priscilla Wilson; Mary Wilson; William L. Wilson (who received property earlier).

WILLIAM GROVES
DOD: August 27, 1805    ADM: Nicholas Allender
H&L: Sarah Groves, widow; Abrm. Groves, son, now deceased; Isaac Groves, son; Asael Groves, son; Sarah Groves, daughter.

BARNABY CONNALLY
DOD: November 16, 1802    ADM: Alexander Rigdon
H&L: Mary Connally, widow; Mary Matson, daughter; Rosanna Hanley, daughter; Catharine Myres, daughter; Eleanor Connally, daughter; Ann Leonard, daughter; Sarah Lawhead, daughter.

ANN OSBORN
DOD: June 11, 1805    ADM: Francis Osborn
H&L: Frances Osborn, sister; Rebecca Osborn, sister.

THOMAS WILSON
DOD: September 10, 1805    ADM: Sarah Jenny and Peter Wilson
H&L: Sarah Jenny, formerly Wilson, widow; Sarah Wilson, now Jay, daughter; Alessanna Cole, daughter; Thomas Wilson, son; Peter Wilson, son; Nathan Wilson, son.

SAMUEL WALLIS
DOD: September 18, 1805    ADM: Aquila Massey
H&L: Sarah Wallis, widow; Randall Wilson, son; Sarah Seth, dau.; Nancy Whiten, daughter; Sarah Offley, daughter.

WILLIAM STALLIONS
    DOD: October 22, 1805     ADN: James Gallion
    H&L: Rebecca Bradley, formerly Stallions, widow; Sarah Powel, daughter; Aquila Stallions, son; Isaac Stallions, son; Samuel Stallions, son.

JOHN CAMPBELL
    DOD: December 11, 1804     ADM: Mary Campbell
    H&L: Mary Campbell, widow; William Campbell, brother; James Campbell, brother; Thomas Campbell, brother; Robert Campbell, brother; Rogers Campbell, brother; Sarah Ashinhorst, sister.

ANTHONY DREW, JR.
    DOD: December 10, 1805     ADM: Priscilla Cole
    H&L: Priscilla Cole, formerly Drew, widow; Susanna Drew, daughter; Aquila Drew, son; Bennet Drew, son.

JOHN GRAVES
    DOD: February 11, 1806     ADM: Robert and Catharine Graves
    H&L: Catherine Graves, widow; Ann Inlows, daughter; Jane Curtin, daughter; Robert Graves, son; Anna Maria Graves, daughter.

CHARLES WORTHINGTON
    DOD: January 7, 1806     ADM: Joseph Worthington & James Johnson
    H&L: Sarah Johnson; Ann Wallis; Charles Worthington; Margaret Worthington; Mary Dallam; Elizabeth Johnson.

JAMES NORRIS, SR.
    DOD: February 12, 1806     ADM: James and Henry Norris
    H&L: James Norris, son; Henry Norris, son; Ann Norris, daughter; Elizabeth Norris, daughter; children of Sarah White, daughter.

ANN WARD
    DOD: February 12, 1806     ADM: Robert Bryarly
    H&L: Hannah McFall, sister; Jane Johnson, sister; Elizabeth Stroud, sister; Richard Ward, brother; James Ward, brother; William Ward, brother.

SARAH KIMBLE
    DOD: February 12, 1806     ADM: Zachariah Kimble
    H&L: Zachariah Kimble, son; Susanna Cowan, daughter; Elijah Kimble, son; Semelia Kimble, daughter.

JOSEPH STILES
    DOD: March 11, 1806     ADM: George Stiles
    H&L: Elizabeth Stiles, widow; George Stiles; John Stiles; Joseph Stiles; Charity Stiles; Edward Stiles; Elizabeth Stiles; Nancy Stiles; Phebe Stiles; Mary Stiles; Samuel Stiles; William Stiles; Rebecca Stiles.

JOHN H. HUGHES
    DOD: August 27, 1805     ADM: James Hughes
    H&L: Ann Hughes, widow; Scott Hughes; Martha Hughes; Ann Hughes; Sarah Mitchell.

ANGUS GREME
    DOD: June 10, 1806     ADM: Mary F. Greme

ANGUS GREME (continued)
   H&L: Mary F. Greme, widow; Frances Greme, daughter; Laura Greme, daughter; Angus Greme, son; Harriott Greme, daughter; Caroline Greme, daughter.

MARTIN PRESTON
   DOD: June 10, 1806    ADM: Rebecca Preston
   H&L: Rebecca Preston, widow; Elizabeth Preston, daughter; Clemency Preston, daughter; James T. Preston, son; Martha Preston, daughter; Benjamin Preston, son; Scott Preston, son.

JAMES McNABB
   DOD: June 10, 1806    ADM: John McNabb and John Jolly
   H&L: Alse McNabb, widow; Catharine McNabb, daughter; Isaac McNabb, son; John McNabb, son; Susanna McNabb, daughter; James McNabb, son; Robert McNabb, son; Daniel McNabb, son.

HOLLIS COURTNEY
   DOD: June 12, 1806    ADM: Eleanor Taylor, formerly Courtney
   H&L: Eleanor Taylor, formerlt Courtney, widow; Hollis Courtney, son; Maria Courtney, daughter; John Courtney, son.

PHILIP COALE (COLE)
   DOD: May 13, 1806    ADN: John Dallam
   H&L: Ann Cole, widow; Cassandra McCoy, daughter; Frances Ford, daughter; Sarah Lukens, daughter; Richard Cole, son; Ann Cole, daughter; Elizabeth Cole, daughter; William Cole, son; Philip Cole, son.

HANNAH CROSSMORE
   DOD: July 15, 1806    ADM: David Lee
   H&L: Robert Way; Jane Way; Sarah Way; John Way; David Way; Hannah Way; Job Way; Phebe Crossmore; William Crossmore.

JOHN BOTTS
   DOD: July 15, 1806    ADM: James Botts
   H&L: Elizabeth Botts, widow; Nancy Hughs; James Botts; Asael Botts; Avarilla Botts.

THOMAS HUSKINS
   DOD: November 18, 1806    ADM: Thomas West and Enos West
   H&L: Mark McGovern; Hannah McGovern, daughter; Elizabeth McGovern, granddaughter; Ann McGovern, granddaughter.

ELIJAH DURHAM
   DOD: August 12, 1806    ADM: John Denbow
   H&L: Mahalah Durham, daughter; Amelia Durham, daughter.

JOSEPH HAYS
   DOD: January 27, 1807    ADM: Archer Hays and John Archer, Jr.
   H&L: Esther Hays, mother of deceased; James Hays, brother; John Hays, brother; Esther McCandless, sister; Archer Hays, brother; Ruth Hays, sister; Mary O'Brian, sister; heirs of Mary Hanna, sister.

JOHN BAXTER
   DOD: February 11, 1807    ADM: James Magness
   H&L: Ann Baxter, widow; Charity S. Baxter, daughter; William Baxter, son.

PRISCILLA GOVER
    DOD: March 3, 1807    ADM: William Cox
    H&L: Heirs of Elizabeth Hopkins, deceased, sister of deceased; Samuel Gover, brother; Robert Gover, brother; Ephraim G. Gover, brother; Heirs of Margaret Dallam, deceased, sister of deceased; Mary Hopkins, sister; Rachel Cox, sister; Cassandra Harris, sister.

RICHARD WARD
    DOD: March 10, 1807    ADM: Joseph Robinson
    H&L: Jane Johnson; Hannah Falls; Elizabeth Stroud; James Ward; William Ward.

ELIZABETH DURHAM
    DOD: August 12, 1807    ADM: Cassandra Hughes, formerly Durham
    H&L: Celia Durham; Elizabeth Hughes; Amelia Binns; Susanna Hillen; Cynthia Hays; John Hellen, grandson; Cassandra Hughes, formerly Durham.

THOMAS STRONG
    DOD: August 12, 1807    ADM: Joseph Strong
    H&L: Sarah Biddison, daughter; Joseph Strong, son; Thomas Strong, son; James Strong, son; William Strong, son; Eliner E. Strong, daughter.

ALEXANDER YOUNG
    DOD: August 13, 1807    ADM: Mary O'Brian, formerly Young
    H&L: Mary O'Brian, formerly Young, widow; Esther Watters, daughter; Robert Young, son; Archer H. Young, son; Thomas Jefferson Young, son; Alexander Young, son; Sarah Young, daughter.

JOHN TOWNSLEY
    DOD: April 11, 1804    ADM: William Mahon
    H&L: Eleanor Townsley, widow; Heirs of Mary Jones, grandchildren of deceased; Heirs of Joseph Townsley, grandchildren of deceased; Heirs of William Townsley, grandchildren of dec'd.

JOHN CALDER
    DOD: September 8, 1807    ADM: Neoma Calder
    H&L: Neoman Calder, widow; William Calder, son; John Calder, son; Sophia Calder, daughter; Matilda Calder, daughter; James Calder, son; Loyd Calder, son.

CHARLES WATTERS
    DOD: October 13, 1807    ADM: Elizabeth Birckhead, formerly Watters
    H&L: Elizabeth Birckhead, widow; Mary Horner Watters, daughter; Ann Osborn Watters, daughter; John Watters, son.

JOHN THOMAS BROWN
    DOD: October 14, 1807    ADN: Elizabeth Bayless
    H&L: Mary Brown, widow of Joshua Brown; Elizabeth Brown, daughter of Mary Brown; John Brown; Mary Brown, daughter of Mary; Augustine Bayless.

AUGUSTINE BAYLESS
    DOD: October 14, 1807    ADM: Elizabeth Bayless
    H&L: Elizabeth Bayless, widow; John Brown Bayless, son; Martha Bayless, daughter.

JOHN PARSONS
DOD: November 3, 1807 ADM: Rebecca Parsons and Jacob Lukens
H&L: Rebecca Parsons, widow; Children of Mary Lancaster, grandchildren of deceased; John Parsons, son; Rebecca Lancaster, daughter; Ruth Smith, daughter; Ann Morford, daughter; Abner Parsons, son; Abraham Parsons, son; Amos Parsons, son; Tace Lukens, daughter.

JOHN WARD
DOD: November 24, 1807 ADM: Benjamin Ward
H&L: Sarah Ward, widow; Sarah Martain, daughter; Elizabeth Ward, daughter; Achsa Ward, daughter; Benjamin Ward, son.

JOHN CARTER
DOD: December 9, 1807 ADM: Samuel Carter
H&L: Rebecca Carter, widow; John Carter, son; Henry Carter, son.

JOHN BARE, SR.
DOD: January 19, 1808 ADN: Jacob Bare
H&L: Barbara Ann Bare, widow; John Bare, son; Catherine Bare, daughter; Jacob Bare, son; Elizabeth Murry, daughter; Samuel Bare, son; Joseph Bare, son.

EZRA SPENCER
DOD: December 15, 1807 ADM: Elizabeth Spencer
H&L: Elizabeth Spencer, widow; Hannah Spencer, daughter; Sally Spencer, daughter; Hugh Spencer, son.

SARAH MITCHELL
DOD: February 10, 1808 ADM: William Mitchell
H&L: William Mitchell, son; Ann Hawkins, daughter.

JAMES ANDERSON
DOD: April 15, 1808 ADM: William Anderson
H&L: Cassandra Anderson, widow; William Anderson, son; Benjamin Anderson, son; Elizabeth Anderson, daughter; James Anderson, son.

DANIEL NORRIS
DOD: June 16, 1808 ADM: Aquilla Norris
H&L: Catherine Norris, widow; James Norris, brother; Thomas Norris, brother; Aquilla Norris, brother; Hannah Fulton, sister; Mary Norris, sister; Susanna Garrettson, sister; Edward Norris, of Edward.

MARTIN T. GILBERT
DOD: December 22, 1807 ADM: Martha and Martin T. Gilbert
H&L: Elizabeth Wilson, daughter; Sarah Gilbert, daughter; Ann Gilbert, daughter; Martha Gilbert, daughter; Julia Gilbert, daughter.

FRANCIS BULL
DOD: March 23, 1808 ADN: William Bull
H&L: John Bull, son; Samuel Bull, son; William Bull, son; Jacob Bull, son; Hannah Bull, daughter; Mary Bull, daughter; Ann Bull, daughter; Frances Bull, daughter.

JOHN BULL
DOD: April 13, 1803 ADN: Henry Watters
H&L: Frances Bull, widow; Samuel Bull, son; William Bull, son;

JOHN BULL (continued)
Jacob Bull, son; Hannah Bull, daughter; Mary Bull, daughter;
Frances Bull, daughter; Ann Bull, daughter.

JAMES LEE
DOD: April 13, 1808      ADM: Parker H. Lee and John Moores
H&L: Priscilla Presbury, wife of George E. Presbury; Mary Moores, wife of John Moores; Blanch Welch, wife of William Welch; Elizabeth Lee, wife of James Lee; Cassandra Gover, wife of Robert Gover; Peggy Smithson, wife of William Smithson.

WILLIAM OSBORN
DOD: May 10, 1808       ADM: Cyrus Osborn
H&L: Avarilla Powell, daughter; Cyrus Osborn, son; Sarah Hollis, daughter; Frances Osborn, daughter; Ann Osborn, daughter; Rebecca Deaver, daughter; James Osborn, daughter.

ELIZABETH HALL
DOD: October 21, 1806   ADM: William McGovern
H&L: Ann O'Daniel, sister; Mary Hill, sister; Alexander Hill, half-brother; Christian Jenkins, half-brother; Sarah Taylor, half-sister; Jane Hooper, half-sister; Samuel Hill, half-brother.

JAMES TINDLEY
DOD: December 9, 1806   ADM: Margaret Tindley
H&L: Jane Tindley, widow; John Tindley; Robert Tindley; Mary Tindley; Alexander Tindley; Margaret Tindley; Hannah Tindley.

PATIENCE DAVIS
DOD: September 8, 1807  ADM: John St. Clair
H&L: Mary Carman, daughter; Elizabeth Baker, daughter; Jane St.Clair, daughter ("as directed by the will of David Davis, deceased").

JOHN PERINE
DOD: March 22, 1808     ADM: Nehemiah and Hannah Armstrong
H&L: Hannah Armstrong, widow; Ann Perine, daughter; Nimrod Perine, son; Martha Perine, daughter.

JACOB GREENFIELD
DOD: June 14, 1808      ADM: Jacob Michael
H&L: Polly Greenfield, daughter; Joseph Greenfield, son; Martha Greenfield, daughter; Henry A. Greenfield, son; Elizabeth Greenfield, daughter; Jacob Greenfield, son.

CATHERINE NORRIS
DOD: March 28, 1808     ADM: John Diven
H&L: Sarah Stewart, sister; John Diven, brother; Elizabeth Cochran, sister.

GREENBERRY DORSEY
DOD: August 9, 1808     ADM: William Lester
H&L: Mary Hanson, daughter; Frisby Dorsey, son; Sally Watters, daughter; Milky Gallup, daughter; Charles Graves, son-in-law; Edward Dorsey, son; Nancy Dorsey, daughter; Josias Dorsey, son; Providence Dorsey, son; Greenberry Dorsey, son; Frances Dorsey, daughter.

THOMAS HUSKINS
DOD: August 10, 1808    ADM: Thomas West and Enos West
H&L: Hannah McGovern; Ann McGovern; Elizabeth McGovern.

RICHARD POOL
DOD: February 16, 1808 ADM: Mary Pool
H&L: Mary Pool, widow; Isaiah Pool, son; Margaret Pool, daughter;
Mary Ann Pool, daughter.

JOHN MARTIN
DOD: August 30, 1808 ADM: Sarah Martin
H&L: Sarah Martin, widow; Ann Martain, daughter.

JAMES KIDD
DOD: February 14, 1809 ADM: Pensely Kidd
H&L: Pensely Kidd, widow; John Kidd, son; Rachel Ward, daughter;
Sally Scarff, daughter; Elizabeth Thompson, daughter; Joshua
H. Kidd, son; Rhode Kidd, daughter; Lettecia Kidd, daughter;
James Kidd, son.

HARMON STUMP
DOD: March 28, 1809 ADM: John Stump
H&L: Elizabeth Jarrett, widow; Elizabeth Stump, daughter; Hannah
Stump, daughter; Mary Stump, daughter; Ann Stump, daughter;
William H. Stump, son.

ELIZABETH BARNES
DOD: February 20, 1810 ADM: Alexander Jeffery
H&L: Cassandra Ray; Adelia Jeffery; Levina Richey; William Barnes.

JAMES PRINE (PERINE)
DOD: February 15, 1810 ADM: Ann Perine and Abrm. Baker
H&L: Peter Perine; Ann Perine; Abrm. Baker.

RACHEL STEPHENSON
DOD: June 13, 1810 ADM: James Stephenson
H&L: James Stephenson, son; Rachel Stephenson, daughter.

MANASSA FINNY (FINNEY)
DOD: June 27, 1809 ADM: James Barnett
H&L: To John Finney's 2 sons; To John Finny's 2 daughters;
Hannah Lowry; John Lowry; Jane Covington.

JOHN WILLIAMS
DOD: August 15, 1810 ADM: William Williams
H&L: Sarah Williams, daughter; another child (name not given).

WALTER BILLINGSLEY
DOD: August 16, 1810 ADM: Robert Bryerly & Barsillia Billingsley
H&L: Ruth Billingslea, widow; James Billingslea, son; Mary
Billingsley, daughter; Walter Billingsley, son; Samuel
Billingsley, son; Barsilla Billingsley, son.

ENOCH JENKINS
DOD: August 16, 1810 ADM: Thomas Gallup
H&L: Ralph Jenkins, son; Elizabeth Jenkins, daughter; David
Jenkins, son; Ann Jenkins, daughter; Catherine Jenkins,
daughter; Kesiah Jenkins, daughter.

PHILIP GILBERT
DOD: March 13, 1810 ADM: Ebenezer Gilbert
H&L: Sarah Gilbert, widow; Ebenezer Gilbert, son; Sarah Gilbert,
daughter; Shadrick Rutledge Gilbert, son; Henry Ruff Gilbert,

PHILIP GILBERT (continued)
   son; Philip Gilbert, son; Elizabeth Gilbert, daughter; Hannah
   Gilbert, daughter.

DAVID BRANSON
   DOD: December 11, 1810          ADM: Elizabeth Branson
   H&L: Elizabeth Branson, widow; Owen Branson, son; Mary Branson,
        daughter; Aron Branson, son; Joshua Branson, son; Priscilla
        Branson, daughter; Ann Branson, daughter; James Branson, son;
        Elizabeth Branson, daughter.

JOSEPH EVERIST
   DOD: March 12, 1811             ADM: Clare Shay, formerly Everest
   H&L: Clare Everest, now Shay, widow; Thomas Standish Everest, son;
        Mary Ann Everest, daughter; John Sevan Everest; son; Clarissa
        Everest, daughter.

ROBERT KIRKWOOD
   DOD: February 12, 1811          ADM: William Kirkwood
   H&L: Jane Kirkwood, widow.

WILLIAM McGRAW
   DOD: April 9, 1811              ADM: Caroline McGraw
   H&L: Caroline McGraw, widow; John McGraw, son; Edward McGraw, son.

ELIZABETH FORWOOD
   DOD: May 7, 1811                ADM: Barnett Johnson
   H&L: Ebenezer Forwood, son; Sarah Forwood, daughter; John Forwood,
        son; Jonathan Forwood, son; Elizabeth Forward, daughter.

ANDREW WILSON
   DOD: May 22, 1810               ADM: Benjamin Wilson
   H&L: Lydia Wilson, widow; James Wilson, son; Benjamin Wilson, son;
        John Wilson, son; Elizabeth Wilson, daughter; Samuel Wilson, son.

JOHN KIMBERLEY
   DOD: February 20, 1810          ADM: James Taylor and Joshua Dulaney
   H&L: Mary Kimberley, daughter, now 18; Martha Kimberley, daughter.

JOSEPH RENSHAW
   DOD: August 10, 1811            ADM: Joseph Renshaw and Aquila Greer
   H&L: Joseph Renshaw, son; Thomas Renshaw, son; Philip Renshaw, son;
        Cassandra Renshaw, daughter; Jane Renshaw, daughter; Elizabeth
        Renshaw, daughter.

JACOB BULL
   DOD: August 14, 1811            ADM: James Quinlan
   H&L: Sarah Bull, widow; Rachel Bull, daughter; Ann Bull, daughter;
        Margaret Bull, daughter; Mary Bull, daughter; Susanna Bull,
        daughter; John Bull, son; Edmond Bull, son; William Bull,
        son; Bennet Bull, son.

ANDREW VANCE
   DOD: August 14, 1811            ADM: Mary Vance
   H&L: Mary Vance, widow; William Vance, son; Robert Vance, son;
        Elizabeth Vance, daughter; Mary Vance, daughter.

WILLIAM PRIGG
   DOD: August 13, 1811            ADM: Edward Prigg and Joseph Prigg

WILLIAM PRIGG (continued)
 H&L: Edward Prigg, son; William Prigg, son; Mary Dawes, daughter; Sarah Johns, daughter; John Prigg, son; Joseph Prigg, son; Martha Gover, daughter; James Dawes, grandson; William Prigg, of William, grandson; Martha Johnson, granddaughter; William Prigg Johnson, grandson; Mary Johnson, granddaughter; Martha Dawes, granddaughter; Martha Prigg Gover, granddaughter; Edward Prigg, of William, grandson; William Dawes, grandson; Henry Johns, grandson; William Prigg, of John, grandson.

HENRY JOHNS
 DOD: August 13, 1811  ADM: Edward Prigg
 H&L: Sarah Johns, widow; Martha Johns, daughter; Nancy Johns, daughter; Henry Hosey Johns, son; William Prigg Johns, son; Mary Johns, daughter.

ASAEL BOTTS
 DOD: August 15, 1810  ADM: James Botts
 H&L: Elizabeth Botts, mother; Sarah Stephenson, sister; Nancy Hughes, sister; Isaac Botts, brother; James Botts, brother; John Botts, brother; Averilla Botts, sister.

ELIZABETH BOTTS
 DOD: August 15, 1810  ADM: James Botts
 H&L: Sarah Stephenson; Nancy Hughs; Isaac Botts; John Botts; Averilla Botts; and mentions Asael Botts, deceased.

MARY COX
 DOD: August 16, 1811  ADM: John Cox
 H&L: William Cox, son; Asael Cox, son; Elizabeth Hawkins, granddaughter; Sarah Pusey, daughter; Mary Brown, daughter; Mercy Ellis, daughter; Rachel Cole, daughter; John Cox, son.

SAMUEL BAYLESS
 DOD: February 12, 1812  ADM: Elizabeth & Zepheniah Bayless
 H&L: Elizabeth Bayless, widow; Phebe Bayless, daughter; Mary Bayless, daughter; Sally Bayless, daughter; Asael Bayless, grandson; Elias Bayless, son; Zepheniah Bayless, son; Samuel Bayless, grandson (son of Elias); Jamima Ramsey, daughter; Mehetable McConkey, daughter; Elizabeth Silvers, daughter.

JANE GREENLAND
 DOD: January 1, 1812  ADM: William Greenland
 H&L: Ann Pogue, daughter; Aquila Greenland, son; William Greenland, son; Elisha Greenland, son; Nathaniel Greenland, son.

ELEANOR BROWNLEY
 DOD: October 20, 1811  ADM: Joseph Brownley
 H&L: To Estate of Catherine Brownley, deceased; Catherine Brownley; James Brownley; Joseph Brownley, Esq.; Thomas Brownley; John Brownley; Nancy McClaskey.

 DOD: January 7, 1812  ADM: Joseph Brownley
 H&L: Ann McClaskey, sister; Joseph Brownley, brother; Thomas Brownley, brother; Catherine Brownley, sister; James Brownley, brother; John Brownley, brother.

RALPH PYLE
 DOD: March 17, 1812  ADM: William Pyle

RALPH PYLE (continued)
   H&L: Sarah Pyle, widow; Sarah Pyle, daughter, and wife of Ralph
        Pyle; John Pyle; William Pyle.

SAMUEL WEBSTER
   DOD: April 16, 1812      ADM: Richard Webster
   H&L: Sarah Webster, widow; Richard Webster, son; Thomas Webster,
        son; Samuel Webster, son; James Webster, son; John Webster,
        son; Isaac Webster, son; Joseph Webster, son.

JANE RENSHAW
   DOD: April 16, 1812      ADM: Joseph Renshaw
   H&L: Joseph Renshaw, brother; Cassandra Renshaw, daughter;
        Elizabeth Renshaw, sister; Thomas Renshaw, brother; Heirs
        of Philip Renshaw, brother.

BENJAMIN WHEELER
   DOD: May 26, 1812      ADM: David Clark
   H&L: Elizabeth Dunnagan, alias Green, daughter; Joseph Lilley,
        who married Sarah, daughter; Thomas Wheeler, son; Giles
        Thomas, who married Ann, daughter; Robert Boarman, who
        married Mary, daughter; Benjamin Wheeler, son; Joseph R.
        Wheeler, son; Michael Wheeler, son; Frances Hellen Wheeler,
        daughter; Charity Tresea Wheeler, daughter.

DANIEL TREDWAY
   DOD: June 23, 1812      ADM: Chrispin & Sarah Tredway
   H&L: Thomas Tredway; Daniel Tredway; Ann Hughes; Edward Tredway;
        Hannah Meads; Susanna Riston; Elizabeth Miles.

JOHN BARE, JR.
   DOD: August 11, 1812      ADM: Jacob Bare
   H&L: Barbara Ann Bare, mother; Catharine Halbfus(?), sister;
        Jacob Bare, brother; Elizabeth Murry, sister; Samuel Bare,
        brother; Joseph Bare, brother.

MOSES CANNON
   DOD: August 11, 1812      ADM: John and William Cannon
   H&L: Thomas Cannon, son; Erasmus Cannon, son; Moses Cannon, son;
        Ann Cannon, daughter; Elizabeth Cannon, daughter; Carlile
        Bare, child of deceased; Atridge Cannon, child of deceased;
        Ellender Cannon, daughter; Mary Cannon, daughter; William
        Cannon, son; John Cannon, son; Rachel Cannon, widow.

ELIZABETH BARNES
   DOD: August 27, 1811      ADM: Alexander Jeffrey
   H&L: Cassandra Ray, daughter; Adelia Jeffery, daughter;
        Lovina Richie, daughter; William Barnes, son.

SARAH BOND
   DOD: September 8, 1812      ADM: Ralph S. Lee
   H&L: Alesanna Lee, daughter; Susan Brinton, daughter.

JOHN MITCHELL
   DOD: December 10, 1811      ADM: John Mitchell
   H&L: Mary Mitchell, widow; Elizabeth Webster, daughter; Elijah
        Mitchell, son; Rachel Webster, daughter; Frederick Mitchell,
        son; Lydia Fulton, daughter; John Mitchell, son; Evan
        Mitchell, son; Mary Vandegrift, daughter.

PHILIP GILBERT
    DOD: August 24, 1811    ADM: Ebenezer Gilbert
    H&L: Ebenezer Gilbert; Henry R. Gilbert; Sally Gilbert; Philip Gilbert; Elizabeth Gilbert.

PARKER GILBERT
    DOD: October 13, 1812    ADM: Elizabeth and Abner Gilbert
    H&L: Elizabeth Gilbert, widow; Sarah Bennett, daughter; Heirs of Parker Gilbert; Priscilla Mitchell, daughter; Heirs of Mary McComas; Abner Gilbert, son; Hannah Hughes, daughter.

JOHN JIBB
    DOD: November 3, 1812    ADM: Joseph Brownley & Wm. Middleditch
    H&L: Mary Butler, alias Ford, daughter; Lucyana Townsley, granddaughter; John Butler, alias Ford, grandson; Harriot Butler, alias Ford, granddaughter; Sophia Butler, alias Ford, granddaughter; Elizabeth Butler, alias Ford, granddaughter; Sarah Butler, alias Ford, granddaughter; Nancy Middleditch, granddaughter.

SARAH PYLE
    DOD: November 3, 1812    ADM: William Pyle
    H&L: Betty Thomas, daughter; Edith Smith, daughter; Mary Thomas, daughter; Abigail Eckhooff, daughter; Sarah Pyle, daughter.

JOSEPH ROBINSON
    DOD: December 21, 1812    ADM: George Robinson
    H&L: Hannah Robinson; George Robinson; Thomas Robinson; John Robinson; Rachel Robinson; Joseph Robinson; Rebecca Robinson; Elizabeth Robinson; William Robinson.

LEVI ALEXANDER
    DOD: April 20, 1813    ADM: Jeremiah Alexander
    H&L: Josiah Alexander, brother; Richard Alexander, brother; Ely Alexander, brother; Herman Alexander, brother; Arametta Biddle, sister; Lydia Alexander, sister; Jeremiah Alexander, brother; Susan Harknas, niece.

GERARD HOPKINS
    DOD: April 20, 1813    ADN: Levi Hopkins
    H&L: Levin Hopkins, son; Frances Hopkins, daughter; Susan Hopkins, daughter; William Hopkins, son; Grace Hopkins, daughter; Amelia Hopkins, daughter.

FRANCIS O'NEAL
    DOD: June 9, 1813    ADM: Thomas W. Ayres
    H&L: Bernard O'Neal; Eleanor O'Neal; Owen O'Neal; mentions John Lee Gibson and John O'Brian; "to the poor of Harford County."

DAVID TATE
    DOD: June 22, 1813    ADM: Peter Vernay
    H&L: Mary Vernay, daughter; Margaret Tate, daughter; Martha Tate, daughter; Samuel Tate, son; James Tate, son; Elizabeth Tate, widow.

THOMAS HALL, JR.
    DOD: June 29, 1813    ADM: Edward Hall
    H&L: Edward Hall; Benedict Hall; George Washington Hall; Carvel Hall.

SAMUEL SMITH
DOD: August 26, 1813　　ADM: William and George Smith
H&L: David Smith, son; William Smith, son; Margaret Dever, daughter; Ann McLaughlin, daughter; George Smith, son; Jane Smith, daughter.

MARTHA ST. CLAIR
DOD: April 20, 1813　　ADM: George St. Clair
H&L: Mary St. Clair; Alazanna St. Clair; Martha St. Clair; Ann St. Clair; also mentions Daniel McComas.

SAMUEL LEE
DOD: August 24, 1813　　ADM: Parker H. Lee
H&L: Mary Lee, widow; Parker Hall Lee, son; Priscilla Presbury, daughter; Mary Moore, daughter; Blanch Welch, daughter; Elizabeth Lee, daughter; Cassandra Gover, daughter; Margaret Smithson, daughter.

SAMUEL RICHARDSON
DOD: June 22, 1813　　ADM: Benjamin Richardson
H&L: Elizabeth Smith; Sarah James; Nancy Heaton; Patty Jones; Benjamin Richardson; Mary Yearly; William Richardson; Samuel Richardson; Susan Richardson.

JOHN HALL
DOD: November 22, 1814　　ADM: Susanna Hall, Elisha Hall, Bernard John Lynch
H&L: Susanna Hall, widow; Sarah Lynch, daughter; Elisha Hall, son; Jane Maulsby, daughter; Ann O'Conor, daughter.

JOHN HAYS
DOD: December 2, 1814　　ADM: Archer Hays
H&L: Esther Hays, widow; Archer Hays; Joseph Hays; Esther McCandless; Mary Young; Alexander Young.

SAMUEL BROOKS
DOD: January 3, 1815　　ADM: Hannah Forwood
H&L: Hannah Forwood, widow; John Brooks, son; Manerva Brooks, daughter; James Brooks, son; Sarah Brooks, daughter.

MARY BLANEY
DOD: March 31, 1815　　ADM: Abraham Ware
H&L: John Blaney, son; Thomas Blaney, son; Joshua Blaney, son; Mary St. Clair, daughter; Ann St. Clair, daughter; Josias Blaney, son; Ruth Blaney, daughter.

SAMUEL FORWOOD
DOD: February 15, 1815　　ADM: Benjamin Rigdon
H&L: Mary Forwood, widow; Samuel Forwood, son; Elizabeth Rigdon, daughter; Mary Preston, daughter; Hannah Forwood, daughter; Children of John Forwood (grandchildren of Samuel), namely, Ebenezer, Sarah, Jonathan and Elizabeth Forwood.

BENJAMIN BENSON
DOD: July 18, 1815　　ADM: Amos Benson
H&L: James Benson, son; Abraham Benson, son; Levi Benson, son; Benjamin Benson, son; Jesse Benson, son; Amos Benson, son; Elizabeth Lawson, daughter; Hannah Branson, daughter.

JAMES OSBORN
DOD: October 10, 1815    ADN: Aquila Deaver
H&L: Cyrus Osborn, brother; Avarilla Poust, sister; Frances Osborn, sister; Sarah Hollis, daughter; Rebecca Deaver, daughter.

JAMES HOLLIS
DOD: October 10, 1815    ADM: William Hollis
H&L: Sarah Hollis, widow; Ann Hollis, daughter; Maria Hollis, daughter; Carvel Hollis, son; Amanda Hollis, daughter; William James Hollis, son.

DAVID BELL
DOD: October 16, 1815    ADM: Peter Vernay and David Bell
H&L: Elizabeth Bell, widow; Lovice Bell; David Bell; Mary Evans; Elizabeth Bryerly; Ann Hawkins; George B. Amos; Martha Amos.

JACOB ALBERT
DOD: October 24, 1815    ADM: Elizabeth Albert
H&L: Elizabeth Albert, widow; Joseph Albert, son; Sarah Albert, daughter; Hannah Albert, daughter; Elizabeth Albert, daughter.

JAMES MICHAEL
DOD: October 24, 1815    ADM: Jacob Michael
H&L: Neoma Michael, widow; Hannah Michael, daughter; Charlotte Michael, daughter; Mary Ann Michael, daughter; William Michael; Matilda Michael, daughter; Susanne Michael, daughter.

HANNAH SMITH
DOD: October 24, 1815    ADM: Nathaniel Smith
H&L: Mary McCracken, daughter; Nathaniel Smith, son; Olive Ingram, daughter; Susanna Gorrell, daughter; Ralph Smith, son; John Smith, son; Hugh Smith, son; Elizabeth Baust, daughter; William Smith, son; Thomas Smith, son.

WILLIAM CANNON
DOD: February 27, 1816    ADM: John Cannon
H&L: Mary Cannon, widow; mentions Joshua Dulany who was guardian to the wife of the deceased.

DAVID E. PRICE
DOD: April 23, 1816    ADM: John Stump
H&L: Rachel Price, widow; John Price, son; Rachel Price, daughter; Margaret Ann Price, daughter.

ZACHARIAH AMOS
DOD: May 21, 1816    ADM: Susanna Amos
H&L: Susanna Amoss, widow; Sarah Amoss, daughter; Levi Amoss, son; Philip Amoss, son; Elizabeth Amoss, daughter; Susanna Amoss, daughter; Ann M. Amoss, daughter.

WILLIAM SIMS
DOD: June 9, 1813    ADM: John Livingston
H&L: Sarah Sims, widow; Robert Sims, son; Francis Sims, son.

WILLIAM LESTER
DOD: February 13, 1816.    ADN: John Webster
H&L: Charlotte Webster, sister; Mary How, sister; Norris Lester, brother; Sophia Dorsey, sister; Sarah McGay, sister.

GABRIEL VANHORN
    DOD:  June 25, 1816        ADM:  William G. Dove
    H&L:  Jesse Vanhorn, brother;  Samuel Vanhorn, brother.

JAMES CURRY
    DOD:  April 15, 1812       ADM:  Elizabeth Curry
    H&L:  Elizabeth Curry, widow;  John Curry, son;  James Curry, son;
          Israel Curry, son.

THOMAS SPENCER
    DOD:  August 14, 1816      ADM:  Mary Shekell
    H&L:  Mary Shekell, widow;  Ann Rebecca Spencer, daughter;
          Avarilla Spencer, daughter.

JAMES DEAVER
    DOD:  August 14, 1815      ADM:  Joshua Deaver
    H&L:  Mable Deaver, widow;  Joshua Deaver, son;  Aquila Deaver, son;
          Sarah Courtney, daughter;  Joseph Deaver;  Mary Taylor, daughter;
          Richard Deaver, son;  Alexander Deaver, son;  George Deaver, son.

WILLIAM BEVARD
    DOD:  August 30, 1815      ADM:  John Livingston
    H&L:  Rebecca Bevard, widow;  Ann Bevard, daughter;  Rebecca Bevard,
          daughter;  Catherine Bevard, daughter;  James Bevard, son;
          William Bevard, son.

JOHN HANSON
    DOD:  June 23, 1812        ADM:  Jonas Courtney
    H&L:  Semelia Lancaster;  John Donovan;  Semelia Osborn's children,
          namely, Susanna Michael, William Osborn, Patty Cole, James
          Osborn, Benjamin Osborn, and John Hanson Osborn;  Children of
          Sarah Courtney, namely, Jonas Courtney, John Courtney, Sarah
          Cole, Milcah Dunn, Thomas Courtney, Cyrus Osborn, Elizabeth
          Courtney, Hanson Courtney, and Matilda Hanson;  Heir at law
          of Elizabeth Thompson, namely, John Thompson.

GEORGE CHAUNCEY
    DOD:  October 8, 1816      ADM:  George Chauncey
    H&L:  George Chauncey, son;  Martha Webster;  Cordelia Chauncey.

JOHN CHAUNCEY
    DOD:  October 8, 1816      ADN:  Aquila Nelson
    H&L:  Garret Chauncey, son;  Sarah Cowan, daughter;  John Chauncey,
          son;  Susan Vansickle, daughter;  Nestor Chauncey, son.

HENRY LAMMOTT
    DOD:  October 15, 1816     ADM:  Christian Hoofman & Jacob Lammott
    H&L:  John Lammott, son;  Moses Lammott, son;  Levi Lammott, son;
          Catherine Lammott, daughter;  Joshua Lammott, son;  Daniel
          Lammott, son;  Barbara Bowzer, daughter.

JAMES ARCHER
    DOD:  August 28, 1816      ADM:  John Archer
    H&L:  Margaret Archer, widow;  John Archer, brother.

MARGARET FULLERTON
    DOD:  December 13, 1815    ADM:  Richard Everitt & Aaron Holland
    H&L:  Alexander Fullerton, son;  Sarah Beard, daughter;  Hannah
          Campbell, daughter;  John Fullerton, son;  William Fullerton,

MARGARET FULLERTON (continued)
   son; Nancy Moor (?), daughter.

EZEKIEL COLE
   DOD: February 11, 1817    ADM: Sarah Cole
   H&L: Sarah Cole, widow; Ann Cole, daughter; Caroline Cole, daughter; Elizabeth Cole, daughter; Ezekiel Cole, son; Jonas Cole, son; William Cole. son; Emmelia Cole, daughter; James Courtney Cole, son.

JOSHUA Ford
   DOD: February 12, 1817    ADM: Martha and William Ford
   H&L: Martha Ford, widow; William Ford; James Ford; Mary Ford; Elizabeth Ford.

JESSE FOSTER
   DOD: March 26, 1817    ADM: John Foster
   H&L: Mary Allender, daughter; Jeremiah Foster, son; Ann Hammitt, daughter; Thomas Foster, son; Sarah Foster, daughter; John Foster, son; Rachel Foster, daughter; Faithful McFaddon, daughter.

JOHN KENNEDY
   DOD: May 21, 1816    ADM: John Kennedy
   H&L: Ann Kennedy, daughter; Elizabeth Kennedy, daughter; John Kennedy, son of Joseph Kennedy.

THOMAS BLANEY
   DOD: April 9, 1816    ADM: Sarah Blaney
   H&L: Sarah Blaney, widow; John Blaney, son; Daniel Blaney, son; Mary Blaney, daughter; Harriet Blaney, daughter; Rebecca Blaney, daughter; Thomas Blaney, son; Anna Blaney, daughter.

PHILIP GARRISON
   DOD: November 19, 1816    ADM: Ann Garrison
   H&L: Nancy Watters; Jefferson Garrison; Ann Canady; Philip Garrison; Joseph Canady; Sarah Hughes; Susanna Amos; Hannah Canady; Betsey Canady; Samuel Garrison; Martha Ralston; Sarah McMasters; Ann Miles.

JOHN HANSON
   DOD: June 23, 1812    ADM: James Courtney
   H&L: Semelia Lancaster; John Donnovan; Children of Semelea Osborn, sister to the deceased, namely, Susanna Michael, William Osborn, Patty Cole, James Osborn, Benjamin Osborn, and John Hanson Osborn; John H. Thompson, only child of Elizabeth Thompson, sister to the deceased; Children of Sarah Courtney, sister to the deceased, namely, James Courtney, John Courtney, Sarah Cole, Milcha Dunn, Thomas Courtney, Elizabeth Ruff, Cyrus Courtney, Matilda Hanson, George W. Courtney, Edward Courtney, and Hanson Courtney.

JOHN CHANCY
   DOD: May 5, 1817    ADN: Aquila Nelson
   H&L: Garrett Chancy, son; Sarah Cowan, daughter; Susan Vansickle, daughter; John Chancy, son; Nestor Chancy, son.

THOMAS AMOSS
   DOD: June 10, 1817    ADM: William and Joshua M. Amoss

THOMAS AMOSS (continued)
 H&L: Ann Amoss, daughter; William Amoss, son; Joshua Miles Amoss, son; Aquila Amoss, son.

JOSHUA FORD
 DOD: February 12, 1818 ADM: Martha and William Ford
 H&L: Martha Ford, widow; William Ford; James Ford; Mary Ford; Elizabeth Ford.

JOSEPH WILSON
 DOD: June 17, 1817 ADM: Thomas Jay
 H&L: Martha Wilson, sister; Hannah Jay, sister; Mary Dallam, sister; Sarah Wilson, sister; Elizabeth Wilson, sister; John Wilson, brother.

RICHARD SPENCER
 DOD: July 1, 1817 ADM: John W. Spencer
 H&L: Mary Gallion, daughter; Sarah McCandless, daughter; William R. Spencer, son; Nancy Spencer, daughter; Elizabeth Miller, daughter; John W. Spencer, son.

MATHEW HAWKINS
 DOD: July 2, 1817 ADM: Elizabeth Hawkins
 H&L: Elizabeth Hawkins, widow; Mary Wilson; Mathew Hawkins, son; Elizabeth Hawkins, daughter; John Hawkins, son; Mary Hawkins, daughter.

SOLOMON BROWN
 DOD: September 30, 1817 ADN: Edward Guyton
 H&L: John Brown, son; James Brown, son; Mary Chambers, daughter; Thomas Brown, son; Solomon Brown, son; Holliday Brown, child of deceased; Margaret Brown, daughter; Samuel Brown, son; Martha Brown, daughter.

JAMES MICHAEL
 DOD: April 28, 1818 ADM: Jacob Michael
 H&L: Hannah Michael, daughter; Charlotte Johnson, daughter; Maranda Smith, daughter; William Michael, son; Susan Michael, daughter; Matilda Michael, daughter; Sarah Simmons, daughter; Keziah Everist, daughter.

JOSEPH LANCASTER
 DOD: May 1, 1818 ADM: Jesse Lancaster
 H&L: Joseph Lancaster, son; Ann Lancaster, daughter; John Lancaster, son.

HENRY RUFF
 DOD: March 1, 1818 ADM: Godfrey Watters
 H&L: Hannah Ruff, widow; John Ruff, son; Joanna M. Ruff, daughter; Richard H. Ruff, son; Henry W. Ruff, son.

MARY CRISWELL
 DOD: April 28, 1818 ADM: James Criswell
 H&L: Isabella Whitson; James Criswell, son; Elizabeth Criswell, daughter; John Criswell, son; William Criswell, son; Mary Criswell, daughter.

ELIZABETH CRISWELL
 DOD: May 5, 1818 ADM: James Criswell

ELIZABETH CRISWELL (continued)
    H&L: Isabella Whitson, sister; James Criswell, brother; John Criswell, brother; William Criswell, brother; Mary Criswell, sister.

JOSEPH DYER
    DOD: October 13, 1817    ADM: Aron Dyer
    H&L: Joanna Dyer, widow; Aaron Dyer, son; Elizabeth Dyer, daughter; Hannah Dyer, daughter; Joanna Dyer, daughter; Phebe Car, dau.; Rachel Parsons, daughter; Joseph Dyer, son; Hester Henderson, daughter.

JOHN KENTLEMYERS
    DOD: October 15, 1817    ADM: Joshua Green
    H&L: Margaret Kentlemyers, widow; Elizabeth Green, daughter; Mary Barnes, daughter; Henry Kentlemyers, son; Ann Levy, daughter; Harriot Kentlemyers, daughter; Alexander Kentlemyers, son.

RICHARD HAWKINS
    DOD: June 10, 1817    ADM: John Hawkins
    H&L: Avarilla Hawkins, widow; Robert Hawkins, son; Elizabeth Barnes, daughter; Thomas Hawkins, son; John Hawkins, son; Ann Smith, daughter; Richard Hawkins, son; Hosier Hawkins, son; Lydia Vandegrift, daughter; Cassandra Courtney, dau.

BENJAMIN AMOSS
    DOD: January 19, 1818    ADM: James B. Amoss
    H&L: Sarah Amoss, widow; Mary Way, daughter; Elizabeth Amoss, daughter; Ann Alderson, daughter; James B. Amoss, son.

ALEXANDER THOMPSON
    DOD: June 16, 1818    ADM: Thomas Thompson & Nathaniel Grafton
    H&L: Priscilla Thompson, widow; Thomas Thompson, son; William Thompson, son; Archibald Thompson, son; Daniel Thompson, son; Alexander Thompson, son; Cassandra Grafton, daughter; Sarah Connolly, daughter; Margaret Wayminn, daughter; Ann Kelsey, daughter; Martha Thompson, daughter.

BENJAMIN AMOSS
    DOD: June 23, 1818    ADM and H&L: Same as January 19, 1818.

HENRY RUFF
    DOD: August 4, 1818    ADM: Henry Ruff & Shadrack Rutledge
    H&L: Richard Ruff, son; Henry Ruff, son; Hannah Rutledge, dau.; Heirs of Sarah Gilbert.

DENIS BOND
    DOD: October 24, 1815    ADM: Mary Bond
    H&L: Mary Bond, widow; Harriott Bond, daughter; Jane Bond, dau.; Frances Bond, daughter; Eliza Bond, daughter; Nicholas M. Bond, son; Elijah J. Bond, son.

HENRY WETHERALL
    DOD: August 27, 1816    ADM: Charlotte E. Birckhead
    H&L: Charlotte E. Wetherall, widow; James Wetherall, son; Henry L. Wetherall, son; Thomas N. G. Wetherall, son; William Wetherall, son; Mathew Wetherall, son.

WILLIAM WARNER
    DOD: November 25, 1818    ADM: Jonathan Warner & John Townsend
    H&L: Phebe Warner of Pennsylvania, mother of William, deceased; Jane Warner, widow; Mary Warner, daughter; Joseph Warner, brother; Mercey Gheen, sister; Hannah Townsend, sister; Martha Warner, sister.

JESSE BENSON
    DOD: March 23, 1819    ADM: Mary and Amos Benson
    H&L: Mary Benson, widow; Joel Benson, son.

MARY LEE
    DOD: August 17, 1819    ADM: William D. Lee
    H&L: Parker H. Lee, son; Mary Moores, daughter; Priscilla Presbury, daughter; Elizabeth Lee, daughter; Cassandra Gover, daughter; Margaret Smithson, daughter.

JOHN CHAUNCEY
    DOD: October 21, 1817    ADM: Garrett Chauncey
    H&L: Susan Vansickle, daughter; Sarah Cowan, daughter; John Chauncey, son; Nester Chauncey, son; Garrett Chauncey, son.

HANNAH THOMAS
    DOD: December 20, 1819    ADM: Jehu Smith
    H&L: Sarah Pyle; Hannah Ecoff; Ann Pyle, daughter of John; Chinworth Poteet; and, "to sundry persons."

JOHN WILLIAMS
    DOD: April 25, 1820    ADM: Eunice Williams
    H&L: Eunice Williams, widow; Julian Williams, daughter; Emily Williams, daughter.

ADAM CLENDINEN
    DOD: February 9, 1819    ADM: John Clendinen
    H&L: Sophia A. Clendinen, widow; mary Clendinen, daughter; Adam Clendinen, son; Amelia Clendinen, daughter.

JOHN CHAUNCEY
    DOD: September 28, 1819    ADM and H&L: Same as October 21, 1817.

ELIZABETH WILEY
    DOD: March 17, 1820    ADM: Vincent Norris
    H&L: James Wiley, son; Jane Duncan, daughter; Mary Norris, dau.

THOMAS WHEELER
    DOD: August 25, 1818    ADM: Benjamin and Ann Quinlan
    H&L: Ann M. Quinlan, daughter; Sylvester Wheeler, son; July A. Bussey, daughter; Ann Dawes, daughter; Charles Wheeler, son; Angus Wheeler, son; Ellen Grindall, daughter; James Wheeler, son; Elizabeth Wheeler, daughter.

JESSE BENSON
    DOD: August 22, 1820    ADM and H&L: Same as March 23, 1819.

ROLAND RODGERS
    DOD: June 27, 1820    ADM: Rowland Rodgers and John Hanna
    H&L: Rowland Rodgers, son; William Rodgers, son; Caroline Thompson, daughter of Elizabeth Mannahan; Ann Hanna, dau.; Jane Rodgers, daughter; Catharine Rodgers, daughter; and, to child of Thomas Rodgers.

HENRY CAVER (CARVER)
  DOD: February 27, 1821        ADM: Moses and Joseph Carver
  H&L: Elizabeth Carver, widow; Moses Caver, son; Aaron Carver, son; Rachel Carver, daughter; John Carver, son; Joseph Carver, son; William Carver, son; Henry Carver, son; George Carver, son; Eliza Carver, daughter; Harriet Carver, daughter.

HENRY WOOLEN
  DOD: March 13, 1821           ADM: William R. Woolen
  H&L: Ann Woolen, widow; Henry G. Woolen, son.

PARKER GILBERT
  DOD: March 15, 1821   ADM: Elizabeth Gilbert & Isaac Perryman
  H&L: Elizabeth Gilbert, widow; Ann Martha Gilbert, daughter; William Gilbert Gilbert, son.

WILLIAM GILBERT
  DOD: March 15, 1821           ADM: Isaac Perryman
  H&L: Elizabeth Gilbert, mother; Ann Martha Gilbert, sister; Mary Harris, formerly Henderson, sister.

WILLIAM MORGAN
  DOD: August 22, 1816          ADM: Thomas S. Chew
  H&L: Elizabeth Chew, daughter; Cassandra Morgan, widow; Sarah Hopkins, daughter; Eleonor Hopkins, daughter; Margaret Morgan, daughter; Mary Hopkins, daughter; Martha Morgan, daughter; Edward Morgan, son; James Lee Morgan, son.

PHILIP GARRISON
  DOD: May 8, 1821              ADM: Ann Garrison
  H&L: Samuel Garrison; Nancy Watters; Martha Rolston; Sarah McMasters; Ann Miles.

JAMES WATKINS
  DOD: January 23, 1821         ADM: Abraham Jarrett
  Distributive shares to negro Fillis and negro Nancy Shaw.

SARAH GILBERT
  DOD: March 9, 1813            ADM: Henry R. Gilbert
  H&L: Ebenezer Gilbert, son; Henry R. Gilbert, son; Sarah T. Gilbert, daughter; Philip Gilbert, son; Elizabeth Gilbert, daughter; Shadrach Gilbert, son;

JAMES M. DAY
  DOD: August 29, 1821   ADM: Richard F. Collis and Sarah Day
  H&L: Sarah Day, widow; Milcha Day, daughter; Priscilla P. Day, daughter; James M. Day, son.

ELIZABETH PITCOCK
  DOD: February 4, 1817         ADM: Jonathan Pitcock
  H&L: Jonathan Pitcock, son; Sarah Pitcock, daughter; Elener Woodward, daughter; Benjamin Pitcock, son; Charles Pitcock, son; Hannah Pitcock, daughter.

CARVIL MATTHEWS
  DOD: November 6, 1821         ADM: Ann Hanson
  H&L: Ann Hanson, formerly Matthews, widow; John Carvil Matthews, son; Milcha Lusby Matthews, daughter; Mary Elizabeth

CARVIL MATTHEWS (continued)
Matthews, daughter; William Levin Matthews, son; Mary Frances Matthews, daughter.

JAMES REED
DOD: July 20, 1819   ADM: Morris Malsby
H&L: Ann Reed, widow; Sarah Reed, daughter; Ann Reed, daughter; Thomas Reed, son; William Reed, son; James Reed, son; Mary Reed, daughter; Hannah Reed, daughter; John Reed, son.

JOSEPH HOPKINS
DOD: December 11, 1821   ADM: Kent Mitchell
H&L: Clemency Gilbert, widow; William Hopkins, son; Mary Ann Hopkins, daughter; John Hopkins, son.

MARY RUFF
DOD: January 29, 1822   ADM: John S. Webster
H&L: Susanna Bolster; Margaret Webster; Mary Webster, Sr.; Mary Watters; Ann Bradford; Charlotte Bradford; Rebecca Webster; Catherine Wilson; Edward Webster; To William Bull's eldest daughter; Daniel H. Skinner; Susanna Wilson; John Skinner Webster; Richard Ruff.

WILLIAM KNIGHT
DOD: January 29, 1822   ADM: Abraham Jarrett
H&L: Sarah Knight, widow; Charlotte Knight, daughter; Ann Maria Knight, daughter; George Knight, son; Elizabeth Knight, daughter; William Knight, son; John Knight, son.

HENRY SPENCE
DOD: February 5, 1822   ADM: Ann Spence
H&L: Ann Spence, widow; Ann Ruth, daughter; William Spence, son; Robert Spence, son; James Spence, son; Rachael Spence, dau.; Henry Spence, son; Ruth Spence, daughter; Serena Spence, daughter; Sarah Spence, daughter; Mary Spence, daughter.

NESTOR CHAUNCEY
DOD: March 5, 1822   ADM: Dr. Joseph Brownly
H&L: Susan Vansickle, wife of Bennet; John Chauncey; Sarah Henderson, formerly Cowan; Heirs of Garret Chauncey.

SARAH HITCHCOCK
DOD: March 12, 1822   ADM: Abraham Jarrett
H&L: Asael Hitchcock, son; William Hitchcock, son; Heirs of John Hitchcock; Isaac Hitchcock; Mary Trulock, daughter; Ann Hicks, daughter; Heirs of Josias Hitchcock, son.

WILLIAM FOARD
DOD: March 14, 1822   ADM: Thomas E. Bond
H&L: Elizabeth Varnal; Rossanna Ford; Susan Foard, daughter of Rossanna; Thomas Ford, son; John B. Foard, son; Joseph Foard, son; Benjamin Foard, son; Isaac Foard, son; Joshua Foard, son; Elizabeth Varnal, daughter; Jane Brannen, daughter; Rossanna Foard, daughter; Robert Ford, son of Thomas; Mary Ford, daughter of Thomas; William Ford, son of John B.; Mary Foard, daughter of John B.; Elizabeth Brannen, granddaughter; George Brannen, grandson; Susan Foard, granddaughter.

SAMUEL GARRISON
   DOD: April 14, 1818      ADM: Ann Garrison
   H&L: Ann Garrison, widow; Martha Scarf, daughter; Ann Garrison, Hannah Garrison, daughter; Samuel J. Garrison, son; James Garrison, son; Philip Garrison, son; John Garrison, son.

JOHN CUNNINGHAM
   DOD: April 9, 1822      ADM: William Allen
   H&L: James Cunningham; William Allen; Francis Asbury, William McKendre and "other members of the Maryland Conference of the Methodist Episcopal Church."

JOHN MAHAN
   DOD: April 9, 1822      ADM: William Mahan
   H&L: Sarah Mahan, widow; Benjamin Mahan, son; Margarett Mahan, daughter; Mary Mahan, daughter; James Mahan, son; Edward Mahan, son; William Mahan, son.

CLARISSA NORRIS
   DOD: May 25, 1822      ADM: Otho Norris
   H&L: Avarilla Norris.

WILLIAM CAREINS
   DOD: November 6, 1821      ADM: William Careins
   H&L: Mary Careins; Margarett Miscimmons; Abraham Rutledge; George Careins; John Careins; Elizabeth West; Margarett Patterson; Ruth Miscimmons.

JAMES O'BRIEN
   DOD: August 28, 1822      ADM: George Wareham and Owen O'Brien
   H&L: Mary O'Brien, widow; Margarett O'Brien, daughter; James O'Brien, son.

CORBIN GRAFTON
   DOD: September 3, 1822      ADM: Martin Grafton
   H&L: Bazilla Grafton; Sarah Grafton, mother; Corbin Streett; Martha Streett; Martin Grafton, brother; Elizabeth Grafton, sister; Ann Grafton, sister; Sarah Grafton, sister; John Grafton, brother.

RUTH RUTLEDGE
   DOD: November 21, 1820      ADM: James Nelson
   H&L: Ruth Hope; Elizabeth Nelson; Susan Mallet; John Rutledge; Nicholas Hope, daughter of Ezra; Hannah Hope, daughter of Ezra; Ruth Hope, daughter of Ezra; Thomas Hope, son of Ezra; and, to negro Hannah.

JOHN HUGHES
   DOD: September 3, 1822      ADM: Samuel Hughes
   H&L: James C. Hughes, son; Henrietta Stokes, daughter; Eliza Stockton, daughter; Ann M. Aldridge, daughter; John L. Hughes, son.

REBECCA WEBSTER
   DOD: August 29, 1822      ADM: Elizabeth Onion
   H&L: Rebecca Young Day; Lloyd Day; Elizabeth Onion; Rebecca Webster Onion; John Webster Onion; Lloyd Day Onion; Agnes Day Onion; Hannah Juliet Onion; Beal Onion; William Young Day; John Young Day.

JOHN DEMOS
    DOD: October 8, 1822     ADM: Edward M. Guyton
    H&L: Aquila Demos; Ruth Demos; John Demos; Thomas Demos; John Demos; Christian Rampley; Catherine Beaty; Eleonora Guyton; Jemima Meads; Susanna Meads; Mary Hughes; Ruth Demos; and, Children of William Demos, namely, William Demos, Mary Demos, David Demos, Susan Demos, Thomas Demos, and James Demos.

JOHN EVERIST
    DOD: August 27, 1822     ADM: Job Everist
    H&L: Mary Everst, widow; Thomas Everst, son; Ezekiel Everist, son; James Everist, son; Sarah Everist, daughter; Mary Everst, daughter; Nancy Everist, daughter; Amos Everist, son; Job Everist, son.

JOHN ELLIS, JR.
    DOD: November 26, 1822     ADM: Jamima Ellis & Marshall Baldwin
    H&L: Jamima Ellis, widow; Elizabeth Ellis, daughter; Samuel Ellis, son; Nancy Ellis, daughter; Lesly Ellis, child of deceased; William Ellis, son; Marshall Ellis, son; and, Pamelia Ellis, daughter.

WILLIAM CALWELL
    DOD: December 3, 1822     ADM: Mary and Thomas Calwell
    H&L: Mary Calwell, widow; John Calwell, son; William T. Calwell, son; Sally E. Calwell, daughter; Mary E. Calwell, daughter; Laura A. Calwell, daughter.

JAMES HILL
    DOD: October 12, 1819     ADM: Hannah Debruler, formerly Hill
    H&L: Hannah Debruller, formerly Hill, widow; William Hill, son; Moses Hill, son; Ricard Hill, son; Patty Hill, daughter; Thomas Hill, son.

JOHN BULL
    DOD: December 10, 1822     ADM: William Bull
    H&L: William Bull, brother; Sarah Osborn, niece.

WILLIAM YORK
    DOD: September 12, 1819     ADM: Elizabeth York
    H&L: Elizabeth York, widow; Mary York, daughter; Edward York, son; Harris York, son; Catherine York, daughter; Statia York, daughter; John York, son; Zelphus York, daughter.

RICHARD HOPE
    DOD: April 8, 1823     ADM: George Careins
    H&L: Jannet Hope, widow; James Hope; Isac Hope; Andrew Hope; Richard Kirkwood; Isac Careins; Richard Hope Careins; Jane Kirkwood; Nancy Kirkwood; Rebecca Careins; Neome Careins; Hannah Thompson.

WILLIAM HALL
    DOD: April 29, 1823     ADM: George W. Hall
    H&L: Sophia Hall, widow; Martha Hall, daughter; Thomas W. Hall, son; George W. Hall, son.

HENRY VANSICKLE
    DOD: 1823     ADM: Aquila Nelson
    H&L: Henry Vansickle, son; Bennet Vansickle, son; Elizabeth

HENRY VANSICKLE (continued)
Vansickle, daughter; Jane Vansickle, daughter; Aquila Nelson, son
of John; Fanny Nelson, daughter; Elizabeth Roberts; Jane Roberts,
daughter; Sally Nelson; Elizabeth Vansickle, widow; Betsy Nelson.

JOHN BARNES
    DOD: June 24, 1823        ADM: Bennet Barnes
    H&L: Elizabeth Barnes, widow; Bennet Barnes, son; John R. Barnes, son.

JOHN ELLIS, JR.
    DOD: September 16, 1823    ADM and H&L: Same as November 26, 1822.

JOHN ELLIS, SR.
    DOD: November 26, 1822     ADM: Jamina Ellis
    H&L: John Ellis, Jr., son; William Ellis, son.

WILLIAM WILSON
    DOD: October 14, 1820      ADM: Clemency Wilson
    H&L: Clemency Wilson, widow; John Wilson, son; Jacob Stallion.

WILLIAM ST. CLAIR
    DOD: October 14, 1823      ADM: Hannah St. Clair
    H&L: Hannah St. Clair, widow; Elizabeth St. Clair, daughter;
    James St. Clair, son; William St. Clair, son.

WILLIAM MARTIN
    DOD: October 7, 1823       ADM: Alexander Hana
    H&L: Catherine Martin, widow; William Martin, son.

WILLIAM THOMAS
    DOD: March 14, 1823        ADM: James Thomas
    H&L: John Thomas; James Thomas; Stephen Rigdon; James Thomas,
    brother; John Thomas, brother; Jane Ward, sister; Elizabeth
    Smith, sister; Hannah Ecoff, sister.

ARTHUR MANAHAN
    DOD: March 23, 1824        ADM: Mary Manahan
    H&L: James Manahan, son; Mary Manahan, widow; Arthur Manahan, son;
    Charlotte Manahan, daughter; Blanch Manahan, daughter; another
    child, not named.

WILLIAM LEE
    DOD: April 13, 1824    ADM: Mahlon Spencer and Ralph Lee
    H&L: Ralph Lee; Mary Reese; David Lee; Sarah Lee; Cabella Lee,
    daughter; Elenor Spencer, daughter; Lloyd Lee, son; Hannah
    Grafton, daughter; Elizabeth Smithson, daughter; Ralph Lee,
    son; Sarah Lee, daughter.

WILLIAM WILSON
    DOD: March 16, 1824    ADM: William D. Lee and Joshua Wilson
    H&L: Pamelia Wilson, widow; Casandra Wilson, daughter; Ann Lee,
    daughter; Rachel Wilson, daughter; Joshua Wilson, son.

ISRAEL MORRIS
    DOD: June 8, 1824         ADM: William Morris
    H&L: William Morris, son; Sarah Morris, daughter; Susana Wilson,
    granddaughter; Asahel Wilson, grandson.

31

MATHEW BIRCKHEAD
    DOD: June 15, 1824    ADM: James Wetherall
    H&L: Charlotte E. Birckhead, widow; Eliza Rearden, formerly Birckhead; Sarah Bateman, formerly Birckhead.

JAMES ST. CLAIR
    DOD: July 26, 1824    ADM: Thomas St. Clair
    H&L: Nancy Smith, daughter; James St. Clair, son; Mary Careins, daughter; John St. Clair, son; Samuel St. Clair, son; Jane Slade, daughter; Baley St. Clair, son; Thomas St. Clair, son; Moses St. Clair, son; William St. Clair, son.

SUSAN WATSON
    DOD: August 11, 1824    ADM: John Stump
    H&L: Rachel Hughes, sister; Mary Mitchell, sister; Elizabeth Trott, sister; Ann Stallings, sister; Abrm. Watson, brother; Walter Watson, brother; Heirs of Margaret Tonyhill.

JOSEPH ELY
    DOD: March 10, 1821    ADM: Amos Ely and Isaac Ely
    H&L: Mrs. Ely, widow; Isaac Ely, son; Amos Ely, son; Ann Ely, daughter; Rebecca Ely, daughter; Martha Ely, daughter; Thomas Ely, son; Joseph Ely, son.

JOHN MILLER
    DOD: 1824    ADN: William F. Miller
    H&L: Edward Miller, son; William Miller, son; John Miller, son; Joseph Miller, son; Elizabeth Wilson, daughter; Mary Bolton, daughter; Ann Haslep, daughter; Rachel Miller, daughter.

DAVID CALWELL
    DOD: August 11, 1824    ADM: Elisah Guyton
    H&L: John Calwell, son; Samuel Calwell, son; Neil Calwell, son; Elisha Guyton; Catherine Calwell, widow; James Calwell.

ANN WHEELER
    DOD: August 24, 1824    ADM: John F. Wheeler
    H&L: John F. Wheeler; George Wheeler; Austin Wheeler; James Wheeler; Heneretta Wilson, wife of Austin; Timothy O'Brien; and, "to the Roman Catholic Church."

SARAH CRAWFORD
    DOD: September 21, 1824    ADM: Samuel Rogers
    H&L: Mary Spencer, daughter; Samuel Crawford, son; William Crawford, son; Sarah Crawford, daughter; Mordicai Crawford, son.

ISAAC WHITAKER
    DOD: April 10, 1811    ADM: Benjamin Everist
    H&L: Margaret Whitaker, widow; John Whitaker, son; Rachel Whitaker, daughter; Amelia Whitaker, daughter; Everett Whitaker, son.

MARGARET BROWN
    DOD: December 7, 1824    ADM: Rowland Rogers
    H&L: Joseph Brown, son; John Brown, son; Absolam Brown, son; Josias Brown, son; Elwood Brown, son; Rachel Brown, daughter.

JOHN CHESNEY
    DOD: August 11, 1825    ADM: William Chesney

JOHN CHESNEY (continued)
 H&L: Ellen Chesney, widow; Anne Chesney, daughter; John Chesney, son.

WILLIAM WILSON
 DOD: March 16, 1824  ADM: William D. Lee & Joshua Wilson
 H&L: Ann Lee, daughter, wife of William D. Lee; Joshua Wilson, son; Pamelia Wilson, widow; Casandra Wilson, daughter; Rachel Wilson, daughter.

WILLIAM TUCKER
 DOD: March 1, 1825  ADM: Eliza Tucker and William Sheckell
 H&L: Eliza Tucker, widow; Mary Tucker, sister; Milly Tucker, sister; Henry Tucker, deceased brother, leaving 3 children, namely, William Tucker, Harriott Tucker (wife of Thomas Cannon), and Rebecca Tucker (wife of William Barling); Nancy Tucker, dec'd. wife of W. Chain, and their son John Chain.

CHARLES GILBERT
 DOD: March 8, 1825  ADM: James C. Gilbert
 H&L: Jarvis Gilbert, son; Elizabeth Gilbert, daughter; James Gilbert, son; Charles Gilbert, son; Comfort Gilbert, daughter; Michael Gilbert, son; Ephraigm Gilbert, son; Ann Anderson, daughter; Mary Weeks, daughter; John Gilbert, son; Taylor Gilbert, son.

ABRAHAM HAYS
 DOD: March 29, 1825  ADM: Thomas Hope
 H&L: Sarah Cooper, now Rutledge, step-daughter of deceased; Gabriel Hays, son; James Hays, son; Mary Hays, daughter; Elizabeth Hays, daughter.

AVARILLA NORRIS
 DOD: June 14, 1825  ADM: Otho Norris
 H&L: Sophia Norris, daughter; Otho Norris, son; Luther Norris, son; Catherine Norris, daughter; John Norris, son; Amanda A. Norris, daughter; George A. Norris, son.

CLARK HOLLIS
 DOD: May 24, 1824  ADM: Richard F. Hollis
 H&L: Mary Hollis, now Norris, daughter; William Hollis Bolster, grandson; James Madizon Bolster, grandson.

THOMAS MORGAN
 DOD: June 14, 1825  ADM: Hannah Morgan
 H&L: Hannah Morgan, widow; Frances Morgan, daughter; Francis I. Morgan, son; Robert L. Morgan, son.

AQUILA McCOMAS
 DOD: September 6, 1825  ADM: Martha McComas
 H&L: Martha McComas, widow; Robert A. McComas, son; Gabriel A. McComas, son.

RUTH BILLINGSLEA
 DOD: October 18, 1825  ADM: William Billingslea
 H&L: Jarvis Gilbert, son; James Billingslea, son; Sarah Bull, daughter; William Billingslea, son; Ruth Billingslea, dau.

JAMES WATSON
 DOD: November 25, 1825  ADM: Mary Watson

JAMES WATSON (continued)
    H&L: Mary Watson, widow; John Watson, son.

HUGH WHITEFORD
    DOD: March 12, 1811    ADM: Michael Whiteford
    H&L: Robert Tarbert; Mary Beatty; Jane Ramsey; Hugh Whiteford; William Whiteford; Mary McKennon; Michael W. McKennon; Thomas McKennon; Rachel McKennon.

ELIZABETH L. WILSON
    DOD: March 1, 1825    ADM: Joseph Davis
    H&L: Elizabeth Kenly, sister; Sarah Kenly, daughter of Samuel; Lemuel Kenly, brother; Kenly Wilson, brother; Elizabeth Kenly, daughter of Lemuel; John James Wilson, brother; William Rite Wilson, brother.

WILLIAM SLADE
    DOD: May 30, 1826    ADM: Abraham Slade
    H&L: Stephen Slade, son; Ezekiel Slade, son; Abraham Slade, son; James W. Slade, son; Elizabeth Slade, daughter.

DELIVERANCE HANNA
    DOD: June 6, 1826    ADM: James Moores
    H&L: James Moores, brother; Sarah Bryarly, sister; Elizabeth Clendenin, niece; James Moores; Samuel L. Moores; Aquilla P. Moores; Parker Moores; Mary E. Bryarly; Susanna Glasgow; Eliza Glasgow; James Glasgow; George Glasgow.

WILLIAM SLADE
    DOD: May 30, 1826    ADM and H&L: Same as May 30, 1826 above.

HUGH WHITEFORD
    DOD: August 15, 1826    ADM: Cunningham Whiteford
    H&L: Ann Whiteford, daughter; Eliza Whiteford, daughter; Jane Whiteford, daughter; Elizabeth Whiteford, widow; Cunningham Whiteford, son.

MATTHEW BIRCKHEAD
    DOD: December 5, 1826    ADM: James Wetherall and Thomas Dorney
    H&L: Charlotte E. Birckhead, widow; Elizabeth Rearden, formerly Birckhead; Sarah Bateman, formerly Birckhead.

ELIZABETH CHEW
    DOD: December 19, 1826    ADM: Samuel Worthington
    H&L: Sarah Worthington's heirs; Cassandra M. Chew; Eliza Chew; Margaret M. Chew.

MARTHA MORGAN
    DOD: February 13, 1827    ADM: Joseph Hopkins
    H&L: Zacheus O. Bond; Elizabeth Chew; Sarah Hopkins; Eleanor Hopkins; Mary Hopkins; Margaret Morgan; James L. Morgan.

GARRETT CHAUNCEY
    DOD: July 11, 1826    ADM: Aquila Nelson
    H&L: Elizabeth Chauncey, widow; John H. Chauncey, son.

CLAUDIUS F. F. DELEPORTE
    DOD: May 15, 1827    ADM: Lewis Marchand
    H&L: Lewis Marchand; Pierre Louis Auguste Marchand.

MARY LONEY
  DOD: May 29, 1827            ADM: Joseph Brownley
  H&L: William Loney Forwood, grandson; Thomas P. F. Forwood, grandson.

JACOB FORWOOD
  DOD: August 23, 1827         ADN: Henry Hall
  H&L: John Forwood, of Jacob's heirs; Joseph Matthews, in right of his wife.

CASSANDRA MORGAN
  DOD: November 28, 1826       ADM: Zacheus O. Bond & John Hopkins
  H&L: Elizabeth Chew's heirs, grandchildren of the deceased; Sarah Hopkins' heirs, grandchildren of the deceased; Cassandra Bond's heirs, grandchildren of the deceased; Eleanor Hopkins, daughter; Mary Hopkins, daughter; James Lee Morgan, son; Margaret Morgan, daughter.

MOSES MAGNESS
  DOD: February 12, 1828       ADM: William Magness
  H&L: John Magness; William Magness; Samuel Magness; James Magness; Amelia Tredway; Benjamin Magness.

JAMES W. HALL
  DOD: November 15, 1826       ADM: Edward Hall and William B. Stokes
  H&L: Sarah Hall, widow; Mortimer D. Hall, son; Mary Hall, daughter; Sophia W. Hall, daughter; Ellen Hall, now Ramsay, daughter; Julianna Hall, daughter.

WILLIAM RICHARDSON
  DOD: March 19, 1828          ADM: Henry G. Watters
  H&L: Thomas Richardson, brother; John Brewer; Rebecca Clark, niece; William Richardson, nephew; Ann Grant, niece; Mary Calvert, niece; Rachel Lowry, niece; Thomas Richardson, nephew; Jacob Richardson, nephew; Catherine Richardson, niece.

WILLIAM BALDWIN
  DOD: April 5, 1828           ADM: Silas Baldwin
  H&L: John Baldwin, son; Silas Baldwin, son; James Baldwin, son.

EDWARD MILLER
  DOD: September 16, 1828      ADM: William F. Miller
  H&L: Adeline Miller, now Allen, daughter; Horatio Miller, son; Joseph Miller, son; Thomas Miller, son.

JAMES FULTON
  DOD: March 10, 1829          ADM: Stephen B. Hanna
  H&L: Mary Ann Hanna, daughter, wife of Stephen B. Hanna; Elizabeth Fulton, widow; Averilla J. Fulton, daughter; Joseph M. Fulton, son; John C. Fulton, son; William Fulton, son; James Fulton, son; Margaret F. Fulton, daughter.

JOHN McFADDEN
  DOD: April 7, 1829           ADM: John McFadden, Jr.
  H&L: Elizabeth McFadden, widow; Jane Hawkins, daughter; John McFadden, son; Elizabeth Harvey, daughter.

SAMUEL RICKETTS
  DOD: April 29, 1828          ADM: Benjamin Ricketts

SAMUEL RICKETTS (continued)
   H&L:  Samuel Ricketts, son; Benjamin Ricketts, son; Thomas Ricketts, son; John W. Ricketts, son; William Ricketts, son; Mary Ann Ricketts, daughter.

ELIZABETH GLASGOW
   DOD:  July 28, 1829      ADM:  James Pannel
   H&L:  Susana P. Glasgow, daughter; Deliverance H. Glasgow, daughter; James Glasgow, son; George Robert Glasgow, son.

THOMAS DENBOW
   DOD:  August 18, 1829      ADM:  Benjamin Toland
   H&L:  Sarah Jackson, daughter; Cassandra Thomson, daughter; Ann Denbow, daugter; Martha Toland, daughter; Bazil Denbow, son; John Denbow, son; Levi Denbow, son; Thomas Denbow, son; Gabriel Denbow, son; Martin Denbow, son.

ELIJAH KELSO
   DOD:  September 1, 1829      ADM:  John Fuller
   H&L:  Frances Kelso, widow; Ann Maria Kelso, daughter; Hannah F. Kelso, daughter.

BENNETT BARNES
   DOD:  October 13, 1829      ADM:  Dr. William Sappington
   H&L:  Hester Barnes, widow; Richard Barnes, son; Henry Barnes, son; William Barnes, son; Lydia Barnes, granddaughter.

MARGARET K. MYERS
   DOD:  October 13, 1829      ADM:  Joshua Green
   H&L:  Elizabeth Green, daughter; Mary Barnes, daughter; Henry K. Myres, son; Ann Levy, daughter; Harriot Whitaker, daughter; Alexander K. Myres, son.

SUSAN WOOD
   DOD:  December 8, 1829      ADM:  George Veazey
   H&L:  William Mahone, son; Thomas Wood, son; Alfred Wood, son.

MARY LOGAN
   DOD:  December 22, 1829      ADM:  Zepheniah Bayless
   H&L:  Elizabeth Logan, daughter; James Logan, son; John Logan, son; Jane Logan, daughter; Mary Logan, daughter.

JOHN WILSON
   DOD:  December 22, 1829      ADM:  Zepheniah Bayless
   H&L:  Sarah Wilson, daughter; John Wilson, son; James Wilson, son; William Wilson, son.

JACOB BAXTER
   DOD:  January 12, 1830      ADM:  Samuel Baxter
   H&L:  Amelia Baxter, daughter; Mary Tredway, daughter; Susannah Pyle, daughter; Amelia Baxter, daughter.

JAMES ST. CLAIR
   DOD:  March 2, 1830      ADM:  Thomas St. Clair
   H&L:  Thomas St. Clair; Nancy Smith; Moses St. Clair; Mary Careins; John St. Clair; William St. Clair; Samuel St. Clair; Jane Slade.

JONATHAN NORRIS
   DOD:  March 11, 1830      ADM:  George and Edward Norris

JONATHAN NORRIS (continued)
   H&L: George Norris; Elizabeth Hudson; Vincent Norris; Charlotte Payne; Athaliah Terrell.

ZACHARIAH AMOS
   DOD: April 13, 1830        ADM: Susanna Amos
   H&L: Susanna Amos, widow; Sarah Amos, daughter; Levi Amos, son; Philip Amos, son; Elizabeth Amos, daughter; Susanna Amos, daughter; Ann M. Amos, daughter.

JAMES McCOMAS
   DOD: March 30, 1830        ADM: Aquila McComas
   H&L: Elisa Hill, formerly Coale, daughter; William Coale, son.

THOMAS TURNER
   DOD: June 1, 1830        ADM: Joseph Turner
   H&L: Mary Turner, widow; Thomas Turner, son; Elizah Turner, son; John Turner, son; William Turner, son; Hannah Turner, daughter; Charles Turner, son; Ann Turner, daughter; Middemore Turner, son; Delia Turner, daughter; Caroline Turner, daughter; Rebecca Turner, daughter; Mary Turner, daugter.

THOMAS STREETT
   DOD: June 22, 1830        ADM: John and William Streett
   H&L: John Streett, son; Roger Streett, son; William Streett, son; Sarah Watt, daughter; Mary Blaney, daughter; Children of son David Streett, namely, Thomas Streett, Isabella Streett, Glenn Streett, Abraham Streett, David Streett, John Streett, Sarah Lorenza Streett, Mary Streett, Robert Streett, Hannah Streett; Children of daughter Elizabeth McClure, namely, Thomas McClure, James McClure, John McClure, William McClure, Seneann McClure, Margaret McClure, Elizabeth McClure, German McClure.

GEORGE TROUTNER
   DOD: August 10, 1830        ADM: Isaac Hawkins
   H&L: David Troutner; Samuel Troutner; Caleb Gallion; and, the mother of the deceased (name not given).

PRISCILLA CHRISTIE
   DOD: September 28, 1830        ADM: Priscilla Christie
   H&L: Charles Christie, son; Eliza Christie, daugter; George S. Christie, son; Henry S. Christie, son; Priscilla Christie, daughter; Heirs of Delia Rodgers, deceased, namely, Elizabeth Hall, Susan Walter, John G. Rodgers, Sophia Rodgers; Heirs of John Christie, deceased, namely, Priscilla Christie, Gabriel Christie, Edward Christie, Sarah S. Christie.

ALEXANDER SUTHERLAND
   DOD: October 12, 1830        ADM: Robert S. Watson
   H&L: Mary Sutherland; Alexander Sutherland; Elizabeth Sutherland; David Sutherland; Margaret Sutherland; Agness Sutherland; Jane Sutherland; William Sutherland; James Sutherland; Frances Sutherland; Elizabeth Sutherland, widow.

JAMES WADSWORTH
   DOD: October 26, 1830        ADM: Lydia Wadsworth
   H&L: Lydia Wadsworth, widow; John Wadsworth, son; James Wadsworth, son; Mary Nelson, daughter; Wiley Wadsworth, son; Samuel Wadsworth, son.

37

ROBERT WATT
   DOD: November 30, 1830    ADM: James Watt
   H&L: Mary Carman, daughter; Joseph Watt, son; Margaret Davis, daughter; Thomas Watt, son; Sarah McClure, daughter; James Watt, son; David Watt, son; William Watt, son; John Watt, son; Sarah Watt, widow; Elizabeth Watt, daughter.

DAVID E. PRICE
   DOD: January 27, 1831    ADN: John H. Price
   H&L: William Wilson, husband of the late widow of David E. Price; Rachel Parker; Miss Margaret Ann Price; John H. Price.

WILLIAM KIRKWOOD
   DOD: 1831    ADM: Richard H. Kirkwood
   H&L: Jane Thompson; Robert Kirkwood, son; Richard H. Kirkwood, son; William Kirkwood, son; James Kirkwood, son; Hannah Kirkwood, daughter; John H. Kirkwood, son.

WILLIAM ARNOLD
   DOD: March 8, 1831    ADM: Henry F. Arnold
   H&L: Harriet Courtney, daughter; Sophia Jackson, daughter; Mary Mitchell, daughter; William Arnold, son; Susan Arnold, widow; Elizabeth Coale, daughter; Henry F. Arnold, son; Delia Mitchell, daughter.

JAMES CARLIN
   DOD: April 5, 1831    ADM: James and Josias Carlin
   H&L: William Carlin, son; Elizabeth Carlin, wife of William; James Carlin, son of Williams; Ruth Carlin, daughter of William; Rachel Carlin, daughter of William; Josias Carlin, son of William; Aaron Carlin, son of William; William Carlin, son of William; Thomas Carlin, son of William.

BENJAMIN RUMSAY
   DOD: July 12, 1831    ADN: Archibald Gittings
   H&L: Miss Neomi Matthews; Miss Henrietta Rumsay; Miss Mary Rumsay; Mrs. Gittings.

RACHEL ANDERSON
   DOD: August 9, 1831    ADM: Thomas Courtney
   H&L: Amos Anderson, son; Mrs. Tredway, daughter; Mrs. Mitchell, daughter; Rachel Loflin, daughter; Mrs. Aquila Tredway, daughter.

GEORGE HERBERT
   DOD: September 6, 1831    ADM: Margaret Herbert, and John Herbert (now deceased)
   H&L: Jane Herbert, widow; Elisa Pritchard, daughter; Mary McGaw, daughter.

BENJAMIN HENDON
SOPHIA HENDON
   DOD: November 15, 1831    ADM: Thomas Hendon
   H&L: Thomas Hendon; Sophia Hendon; Mary Standiford; Joshua Hendon; Josias Hendon; James Hendon.

JOHN THOMAS
   DOD: January 3, 1832    ADM: James Thomas
   H&L: Jane Ward, sister; James Thomas, brother; John Smith,

JOHN THOMAS (continued)
nephew; Mary Smith, niece; Mary Ann Ecoff, niece; Ann Ecoff,
niece; Susanna Ecoff, niece.

JOHN WATTERS
DOD: November 15, 1831        ADM: Esther Watters
H&L: Esther Watters, widow; Walter Watters, son; Mary Y.
Watters, daughter; William H. Watters, son; Robert A.
Watters, son; Esther Y. Watters, daughter; Thomas G.
Watters, son; John F. Watters, son; Sarah E. Watters,
daughter; Edwin D. Watters, son; Susan J. Watters,
daughter; John W. Watters, son.

JAMES A. HUSTON
DOD: March 6, 1832            ADM: John McGaw
H&L: John Huston, brother; Elizabeth Criswell, sister; Samuel
Huston, brother; William Huston, brother; Margaret Hillis,
sister; Robert Huston, brother; Hamilton Huston, brother;
Lavina Enlows, sister; Sarah Irvin, sister.

ROBERT MONTGOMERY
DOD: March 20, 1832           ADM: Nathaniel West
H&L: Lee W. Montgomery; Samuel Montgomery; Ruth Montgomery;
Maranda Montgomery; John Montgomery; Jonathan Montgomery.

JAMES QUINLAN
DOD: April 3, 1832            ADM: Henry Quinlan
H&L: Susanna Quinlan, widow; Henry Quinlan, son; Isaac Quinlan,
son; William M. Quinlan, son; Susanna Quinlan, daughter.

SUSAN VANSICKLE
DOD: April 3, 1832            ADM: John Chauncey
H&L: Sarah Henderson, wife of George, and sister of the deceased;
John Chauncey, brother; John H. Chauncey, nephew.

JOHN MOORES
DOD: May 23, 1832             ADM: James Moores
H&L: Mary Moores, widow; James Moores, son; Samuel Lee Moores,
son; Aquila P. Moores, son; Parker Moores, dec'd., son;
Mary E. Bryarly, granddaughter; Elizabeth Moores, daughter.

WILLIAM TUCKER
DOD: October 9, 1832    ADM: Rebecca Tucker & William G. Dove
H&L: Rebecca Tucker, widow; William Tucker, son; Thomas H.
Tucker, son.

THOMAS S. CHEW
DOD: December 4, 1832         ADM: Samuel Worthington
H&L: Elizabeth Chew, widow; Cassandra M. Chew, daughter; Elisa
M. Chew, daughter; Margaret M. Chew, daughter; Heirs of
Sarah Worthington, daughter of Thomas S. Chew, namely, Thomas
Worthington, Henry Worthington, Priscilla Worthington, and
William Worthington.

HUGH PORTER
DOD: December 18, 1832        ADM: Thomas Hope
H&L: Mrs. Porter, widow; Hugh Porter, son; Jane Porter, daughter;
Peggy Porter, daughter; Elisa Porter, daughter.

WALTER BULL
  DOD: February 5, 1833          ADM: Sarah Bull
  H&L: Sarah Bull, widow; Sarah Enlows, daughter; Walter Bull,
       son; John E. Bull, son; William E. Bull, son; Ruth Lee,
       daughter.

JOHN DEMOSS
  DOD: January 5, 1833           ADM: Edward M. Guyton
  H&L: Thomas Demoss, son; Christianna Rampley, daughter;
       Catherine Beatty, daughter; Jamima Meads, daughter;
       John Demoss, son; Aquila Demoss, son; Mary Hughes,
       daughter; Ruth Tredway, daughter; Heirs of William
       Demoss, deceased, namely, William Demoss, Mary Bankhead,
       David Demoss, Susanna McCubbin, Thomas Demoss, and James
       Demoss (grandchildren of John Demoss); Eleanor Guyton,
       daughter; Susanna Meads, daughter.

WILLIAM E. MILLER
  DOD: May 14, 1833              ADM: Richard N. Allen
  H&L: Adeline F. Allen; Horatio N. Miller; Joseph W. Miller;
       Thomas C. Miller.

MARY WATTERS
  DOD: January 8, 1833           ADM: William Watters
  H&L: Mary Watters, niece; Sarah Harryman, niece; Elizabeth
       Harryman, niece; Sarah Harryman, sister.

BENJAMIN RUMSAY
  DOD: June 8, 1833              ADN: Martha Gittings
  H&L: Miss Neomi Matthews; Miss Henrietta Rumsay; Miss Mary
       Rumsay; Mrs. Martha Gittings.

ARCHER HAYS
  DOD: June 4, 1833              ADM: Thomas A. Hays & Stevenson Archer
  H&L: Mrs. Hays, widow; Thomas A. Hays; Pamelia B. Hays; John
       Hays; Elizabeth S. Jarrett; Nathaniel W. S. Hays; Henry
       H. B. Hays; Harriet B. Hays; William S. Hays; Ellen H.
       Davis, daughter of Mary Davis, deceased.

HENRY STUMP
  DOD: June 18, 1833             ADN: Thomas Archer
  H&L: Thomas Smith; William Smith; Henry Smith; Reubin Smith;
       Hugh Smith; Hannah Smith; Betsy Smith; Mary Smith; Hetty
       Smith; Martha Smith.

TUDER CHOCKE
  DOD: July 2, 1833              ADM: John Kean
  H&L: Carvel Chocke; Mary Davis, granddaughter; Elizabeth Wilmer,
       granddaughter; Sarah Hughes, granddaughter; Carvel Davis,
       grandson.

JESSE TAYLOR
  DOD: October 15, 1833          ADM: Cooper S. Boyd
  H&L: Sarah McCally, daughter; Frances Crawford, daughter;
       Milcha Boyd, daughter.

JAMES COLE
  DOD: October 15, 1833          ADM: Catherine Cole
  H&L: Catherine Cole, widow; James Cole, of Benjamin, nephew.

GEORGE CUNNINGHAM
    DOD: November 19, 1833    ADM: Ann Cunningham
    H&L: Ann Cunningham, widow; Lloyd Cunningham, son; George Cunningham, son; Sarah Ann Jarvis, daughter; Elizabeth Cunningham, daughter; Merican Cunningham, child of deceased; Kesiah Cunningham, daughter; Crispin Cunningham, son; Isabella Cunningham, daughter; Oliver Cunningham, son; Daniel Cunningham, son.

WILLIAM GLADDEN
    DOD: November 19, 1833    ADM: Jacob Gladden
    H&L: Hannah Gladden, daughter; Nancy Haden, daughter; John Gladden, son; Jacob Gladden, son; William Gladden; Mary Gladden; Jane Watt; Elizabeth Streett.

JOHN PATTERSON
    DOD: December 10, 1833    ADM: Martha Patterson
    H&L: Martha Patterson, widow; Mary Patterson, daughter; John N. Patterson, son; Samuel Patterson, son; Martha A. Patterson, daughter.

ELI HATTON
    DOD: December 17, 1822    ADM: Averilla Hatton
    H&L: Averilla Hatton, widow; Elizabeth P. Hatton, daughter, who married Benjamin Standiford; Rebecca Ann Hatton, daughter.

ELIZABETH CAIN
    DOD: May 7, 1833    ADM: Samuel Smith
    H&L: Mary Cain; Mary O'Brien; Jane Guyton; Sarah Cain; Nancy Haflin; Catherine McLaughlin; Susanne Haughey; Jane Cunningham; James Fickey; Thomas Lilley; James Lilley; George Lilley; Thomas S. Bond; Rev. Timothy O'Brien; Owen Keenan.

BARNET JOHNSON
    DOD: January 27, 1834    ADM: John Forwood
    H&L: Ann E. Johnson, daughter; John Johnson, son; James Johnson, son.

SAMUEL S. BARRON
    DOD: January 7, 1834    ADM: Nathan M. Barron
    H&L: Susanna Barron, widow; John M. Barron, son; Benjamin N. Barron, son; Merick Barron, son; Nathan M. Barron, son; Samuel H. Barron, son; Cornelia E. Barron, daughter; Catherine Ann Barron, daughter.

ROBERT MORGAN
    DOD: February 4, 1834    ADM: Joseph Coudon
    H&L: Elizabeth Hawkins Elliott, daughter; Elizabeth H. Elliott for William Morgan Elliott; Elizabeth Morgan, widow; Kesiah Elliott; Harriot Elliott; Eliza Ann Elliott; Thomas Morgan Elliott; Benjamin Sergant Elliott.

THOMAS JEFFERY
    DOD: February 18, 1834    ADM: James Pannell
    H&L: Alexander Jeffery, brother; Martha Thompson, niece; Mary Williams, daughter (wife of William Williams); Telitha Mitchell, daughter (wife of John Mitchell); Thomas Jeffery, son; $25 each to negro Harry and negro Grace.

MARTHA DORSEY
    DOD: March 4, 1834    ADN: James Dorsey
    H&L: Milcha Dorsey, daughter; Prudence Dorsey, daughter;
    John Dorsey, son; Salina Dorsey, daughter; James H.
    Dorsey, son.

EDWARD KAIN
    DOD: March 12, 1834    ADM: Thomas Kain
    H&L: Edward Kain, son; Catherine Kain, daughter; William
    Kain, son; Thomas Kain, son; "to Roman Catholic Priest
    for the poor of his congregation."

JAMES BOSLEY
    DOD: August 13, 1833    ADM: Joseph Bosley
    H&L: Vincent Bosley; Mary Bosley; Elizabeth Heaton; James
    Bosley, Jr., nephew; Willey E. Bosley, niece; Joseph
    Bosley.

WILLIAM GLADDEN
    DOD: April 15, 1834    ADM: Jacob Gladden
    H&L: Jacob Gladden, son; William Gladden, son; Mary Gladden,
    daughter; Jane Watt, daughter; Elizabeth Street, dau.;
    Hannah Gladden, daughter; Nancy Gladden, daughter.

JAMES WILLIAMS
    DOD: May 27, 1834    ADM: Letitia Williams
    H&L: Letitia Williams, widow; Francis Williams, only child.

JOHN ROUSE
    DOD: June 3, 1834    ADM: Sarah and Christopher C. Rouse
    H&L: Sarah Rouse, widow; Elizabeth Onion, daughter; Rebecca
    Rouse, daughter; Christopher C. Rouse, son; Margaret A.
    Rouse, daughter; Mary L. Rouse, daughter.

JOSHUA DULANY
    DOD: June 10, 1834    ADM: Aquila Dulany
    H&L: Joshua Dulany, son; Aquila Dulany, son; Mary Dulany, dau.

WILLIAM AMOS
    DOD: June 24, 1834    ADM: Lemuel Amos
    H&L: Elizabeth Amos, widow; Heirs of Sarah Morgan; Hannah
    Harlon; Ann Cunningham; Martha Dillon; Thomas Amos'
    son (grandchild of deceased); Susanna Amos; Elizabeth
    Amos; Samuel B. Hugo; Elizabeth Trimble.

ASAEL BAILEY
    DOD: June 24, 1834    ADM: Amos Gilbert
    H&L: Mary Bailey, widow; Elizabeth Bailey, daughter;
    William A. Bailey, son; James H. Bailey, son; Charles
    L. Bailey, son.

DAVID E. PRICE
    DOD: July 22, 1834    ADM: John H. Price
    H&L: William Wilson, husband of the late widow of David Price;
    Rachel Parker, daughter; Margaret Ann Gilpin, daughter;
    John H. Price, son.

BENJAMIN SILLOCK
    DOD: December 2, 1834    ADM: Nathaniel Sillock

BENJAMIN SILLOCK (continued)
    H&L:    Hannah Sillock, widow; Nathaniel Sillock; Honford Sillock; Benjamin Sillock.

HENRIETTA WHEELER
    DOD:    December 16, 1834    ADM: Henry P. Wheeler & Carvel H. Prigg
    H&L:    Christianna Prigg; Henry P. Wheeler; Elizabeth Wheeler; Mary Wheeler; Caroline Wheeler.

PACA SMITH
    DOD:    January 16, 1835    ADM: Mrs. Margaret Smith
    H&L:    Margaret Smith, widow; Children of Dr. William M. Dallam (the deceased's nephews and nieces), namely, Josias W. Dallam, John P. Dallam, Frances C. Dallam, Benjamin R. Dallam, and William H. Dallam; To deceased's nephews, William Smith, Augustus Smith, George Smith, Jacob Smith, Winston Smith, and Edward Smith.

JOHN POTEET
    DOD:    January 20, 1835    ADM: Jesse Poteet
    H&L:    Jesse Poteet, brother; Thomas Poteet, brother; William Poteet, brother; James Poteet, brother.

SAMUEL S. BARRON
    DOD:    January 27, 1835    ADM: Nathan M. Barron
    H&L:    Susanna Barron, widow; John M. Barron, son; Merrick Barron, son; Benjamin Barron, son; Cornelia E. Barron, daughter; Catherine A. Barron, daughter; Samuel H. Barron, son; Nathan M. Barron, son.

WILLIAM McMATH
    DOD:    March 3, 1835    ADM: Mary Jordan
    H&L:    Mary McMath; Sophia Jordan, niece; Wakeman Bryarly, son of Dr. Bryarly; Sarah Bryarly; Mary Jordan; Jane Johnson; William M. Jordan.

ADAM CLENDENIN
    DOD:    April 28, 1835    ADM: John Clendenin
    H&L:    Sophia A. Clendenin, now Ritaker, widow; Mary Clendenin, now Valient, daugter; Amelia Clendenin, now Kane, daughter; and, Adam Clendenin, son.

JACOB BROWN
    DOD:    November 18, 1834    ADM: Benjamin Chauncey
    H&L:    Fenton M. Brown; Thomas Brown; Susan Brown.

JOHN ST. CLAIR
    DOD:    September 29, 1835    ADM: Elizabeth St. Clair
    H&L:    Elizabeth St. Clair, widow; James St. Clair, son; Ann St. Clair, daughter; Jane St. Clair, daughter; Caroline St. Clair, daughter; Mary St. Clair, daughter; Elizabeth St. Clair, daughter.

DANIEL GALLUP
    DOD:    December 15, 1835    ADM: Oliver Gallup
    H&L:    Catherine Gallup; Maria Gallup; Rachel Gallup; Oliver Gallup; Henry Gallup.

JESSE ALLEN
    DOD:    January 12, 1836    ADM: Walter Jarvis

43

JESSE ALLEN (continued)
 H&L: Ann Jarvis; Harriett Stephens; John Allen's heirs and widow.

JOHN CANNON
 DOD: April 26, 1836 ADM: Noble Cannon
 H&L: John Cannon, son; Mary Taylor, daughter.

JOHN DEMOSS
 DOD: May 10, 1836 ADM: Edward M. Guyton
 H&L: Thomas Demoss, son; Christianna Rampley, daughter; Catherine Beatty, daughter; Jamima Meads, daughter; John Demoss, son; Aquila Demoss, son; Mary Hughes, daughter; Ruth Tredway, daughter; Heirs of William Demoss, deceased; Eleanor Guyton, daughter; Susanna Mead, daughter.

JAMES JERVIS
 DOD: June 7, 1836 ADM: John Jervis
 H&L: Sarah Ann Jervis, widow; Eliza Ann Jervis, daughter; Cornelia F. Jervis, daughter; Elizabeth Ann Jervis, dau.

JOHN ROUSE
 DOD: June 14, 1836 ADM: Sarah & Christopher C. Rouse
 H&L: Sarah Rouse, widow; Elizabeth Onion, daughter; Rebecca Rouse, daughter; Christopher C. Rouse, son; Margaret A. Rouse, daughter; Sarah J. Birckhead, daughter; Mary L. Rouse, daughter.

LLOYD B. HIPKINS
 DOD: July 26, 1836 ADM: Charles G. Hipkins
 H&L: Charles G. Hipkins, brother; Caleb M. Hipkins, brother; Eliza Hipkins, sister; Emma Hipkins, sister; William L. Hipkins, brother; Joshua D. G. Hipkins, brother; Rhoda Hipkins, sister; Thomas H. G. Hipkins, brother.

JOHN FORWOOD
 DOD: August 2, 1836 ADM: Parker Forwood
 H&L: George Rider; James Harvey; William J. McElhiney; John Preston; Joseph Parker; Samuel Stump; Ducket Stump.

WILLIAM SHECKELL
 DOD: August 10, 1836 ADN: Samuel H. Birckhead
 H&L: Ann O. Sheckell, widow; Eleanor Sheckell; Oleavia Sheckell; Edward T. Sheckell; James W. Sheckell; Ann Sheckell.

WILLIAM M. LANSDALE
 DOD: November 3, 1835 ADM: John H. Price
 H&L: Eliza Lansdale, widow; Maria M. Lansdale, daughter; Philip Lansdale, son; Cornelia Lansdale, daughter; Caroline Lansdale, daughter.

ANDREW CARMAN
 DOD: August 16, 1836 ADM: Esther Carman
 H&L: Esther Carman, widow; Thomas Carman; John Carman; David Carman; Patience Carman; Hannah Carman; Andrew Carman; Mary Rutter; Ann Carman; To Nathan Carman's heirs; Elijah Carman; Esther Kennedy; Nancy Chappell; Caleb Carman; Robert Carman.

ELIZABETH OSBORN
    DOD: August 23, 1836     ADM: Otho Scott
    H&L: Thomas H. Garrettson; James A. Garrettson; Richard F. Garrettson; William E. Garrettson.

JOHN STUMP
    DOD: September 20, 1836     ADM: John W. Stump
    H&L: Cassandra Stump, widow; Ann Archer, daughter; Priscilla Stump, daughter; Mary Williams, daughter; John W. Stump, son; Hannah C. Williams, daughter; Herman Stump, son.

WILLIAM G. DOVE
    DOD: September 27, 1836     ADM: Martha G. Dove
    H&L: Martha G. Dove, widow; Elizabeth Cato; Mary A. Dove; Marmaduke Dove; Thomas W. Dove.

ALEXANDER HANNA
    DOD: October 11, 1836     ADM: John Hanna
    H&L: Jane Watters; John Watters; Elizabeth Fulton; Mary Rogers; Sarah Fulton; Alexander Hanna; Robert Hanna; William Hanna; Stephen B. Hanna; Jane McGaw.

THOMAS DEMOSS
    DOD: October 25, 1836     ADM: David Pyle
    H&L: Sarah Demoss, widow; Mary Susanna Demoss.

ANN MICHAEL
    DOD: October 25, 1836     ADM: Daniel Michael
    H&L: William Michael; Susan Osborn; Martha (no last name given); Bennet Michael; Jacob Michael; Daniel Michael; George Michael; Henry Michael; Elizabeth Miller; Heirs of William Michael, namely, Martha, Ann, Caleb, Owne and Lovenia; Heirs of Martha (no last name given); Mahala Mitchell; Harriot Mitchell; Bennet Mitchell; Daniel Mitchell; Heirs of Ann Buckingham, deceased.

SARAH TREDWAY
    DOD: November 1, 1836     ADM: Daniel Tredway
    H&L: Chinworth Tredway; Daniel Tredway; Thomas Tredway; Ruth Tredway; Sarah Tredway; John Tredway; Crispin Tredway; John Tredway, brother to the deceased.

CHARLTON M. WALTHAM
    DOD: November 22, 1836     ADM: William P. Taylor
    H&L: Hester Waltham, widow; Charlton Walthom; Susan Walthom; Augustus Walthom.

MARY B. BROWN
    DOD: January 24, 1837     ADM: Samuel Bradford
    H&L: Sarah G. Husband; William Brown; Heirs of Thomas Brown, deceased; Mary Brown.

JOHN CHISHOLM
    DOD: January 31, 1837     ADM: Mary Saunders, formerly Chisholm
    H&L: Mary Chisholm, now Saunders, widow; John Chisholm; Elizabeth A. Fareall; Charles T. Chisholm.

JEHU BLACKBURN
    DOD: February 14, 1837     ADM: Hugh Jones
    H&L: Jehu M. Blackburn; Hester Ann Sidwell.

THOMAS JOHNSON
    DOD: March 22, 1837         ADM: Ann Johnson
    H&L: Ann Johnson, widow; John L. Johnson; Barnet Johnson; James
         Johnson; Margaret L. Clark; Thomas Johnson; Sarah A. Johnson;
         Robert Johnson.

JOHN CANNON
    DOD: March 14, 1837          ADM: Noble Cannon
    H&L: John Cannon; Mary Taylor.

THOMAS GALLUP
    DOD: April 4, 1837           ADM: Augustus W. Bradford
    H&L: Catherine Gallup, widow; Eldirdge Gallup, son; Edward Gallup,
         son; Thomas Gallup, son.

ISAAC BOTTS
    DOD: April 18, 1837          ADM: William Stephenson
    H&L: Isaac Botts, son; John Botts, son; Elizabeth Botts, daughter;
         Averilla Botts, daughter.

ELIZABETH P. ARCHER
    DOD: April 25, 1837          ADM: John T. Archer
    H&L: Cordelia P. Archer; John T. Archer; Robert H. Archer; James
         P. Archer.

JAMES SMITH
    DOD: August 8, 1837          ADM: Sarah and James H. Smith
    H&L: Sarah Smith, widow; Ann Warner; William Smith; Daniel Smith;
         Sarah Smith; Thomas Smith; Elizabeth Smith; James H. Smith;
         Ruth Smith; George Smith; Joseph Smith; David Smith.

JACK DURBIN
    DOD: August 22, 1837         ADM: Bonaparte Durbin
    H&L: Grace Wilson; Hannah Hopkins; Susan Giles; Harriot Wesley;
         Mary Presbury; Isabella Kennard; Bonaparte Durbin; Eliza
         Young; Christian Durbin.

JOHN STUMP
    DOD: September 19, 1837      ADM: John W. Stump
    H&L: Cassandra Stump, widow; Ann Archer; Priscilla Stump; Mary
         Williams; John W. Stump; Hannah C. Williams; Herman Stump.

GLENN STREETT
    DOD: November 7, 1837        ADM: Kesiah Streett
    H&L: Kesiah Streett, widow; Isabella Butler, sister; Thomas
         Streett, brother; Abraham Streett, brother; Mary Streett,
         sister; Lorenza Gorsuch, sister; Robert Streett, brother;
         David Streett, brother; Hannah Ashton; sister; John Streett,
         brother.

THOMAS GALLUP
    DOD: November 21, 1837   ADM and H&L: Same as April 4, 1837.

JOHN C. TIMMONS
    DOD: January 16, 1838        ADM: Benjamin Pitcock
    H&L: Elizabeth Timmons, widow; Thomas Timmons; Julian Timmons;
         Wesley Timmons; Joseph E. Timmons; Sarah Timmons.

WILLIAM M. LANSDALE
    DOD: November 3, 1835        ADM: John H. Price

WILLIAM M. LANSDALE (continued)
    H&L: Eliza Lansdale, widow; Maria M. Lansdale; Philip Lansdale; Cornelia Lansdale; Caroline Lansdale.

WILLIAM TUCKER
    DOD: January 13, 1835    ADM: Rebecca Tucker
    H&L: Rebecca Tucker, widow; William Tucker, son; Thomas H. Tucker, son.

HENRY MARTIN
    DOD: May 15, 1838    ADM: Abraham Martin
    H&L: Ceney Everitt; Abraham Martin; Ann Martin; Samuel Martin; Elizabeth Martin; To Mary Swift's heirs, grandchildren of the deceased; John Martin; Cassandra McComas.

GEORGE SMITH
    DOD: May 29, 1838    ADM: Samuel Smith
    H&L: Ann Smith, widow; John Smith; William Smith; Ann Smith; Samuel Smith; Richard Smith; Averilla Smith; Robert Smith; George Smith; Cassandra Smith.

JOSIAS HALL
    DOD: May 29, 1838    ADM: John C.C. Hall and George J.O. Hall
    H&L: Louisa E. Hall; Mary C. Hall; Averilla J. Hall; Adeline B. Hall; John C.C. Hall; George J.O. Hall; Martha M. Lemmon; Sophia S. Hall.

WILLIAM LEE
    DOD: January 22, 1837    ADM: James Moores and Joshua Wilson
    H&L: Ann Lee, widow; Pamelia E. Lee; Cassandra W. Lee; Blanch H. Lee; Frances A. Lee; Mary P. Lee.

JOHN O'NEILL
    DOD: March 12, 1839    ADM: William O'Neill
    H&L: Parker Mitchell, son-in-law; John O'Neill; Matilda Wood; William O'Brian; William O'Neill; To Owen O'Brien's heirs, grandchildren of the deceased; Mary O'Neill; Jane Mitchell; James Miller; James Davis; Mary Douelle; To negro Boy ($).

THOMAS COURTNEY
    DOD: July 23, 1839    ADM: George W. Courtney
    H&L: Sarah Courtney, widow; Hollis Courtney; Thomas Courtney, grandson; William Courtney, grandson; America Courtney, grandson; Thomas Courtney; George W. Courtney; Sarah Cole; Milcha Donn; Edward Courtney; Heirs of Matilda Hanson.

ANN ROBERTS
    DOD: August 6, 1839    ADM: Mary E. Amos and Isaac Amos
    H&L: James Amos, grandson; Mary E. Amos, daughter; Caroline Roberts, daughter.

JACOB GALLION
    DOD: 1839    ADM: Mary M. Gallion
    H&L: Mary M. Gallion, widow; Joshua F. Gallion; Martha E. Gallion; Garrett G. Gallion; Jacob H. Gallion; Mary S. Gallion.

WILLIAM G. DOVE
    DOD: August 13, 1839    ADM: Martha G. Billingslea and James Paul
    H&L: Martha G. Billingslea, formerly widow of the deceased; Elizabeth Cato; Mary A. Dove; Marmaduke Dove.

ELIZABETH MONTGOMERY
  DOD: September 3, 1839    ADM: James Montgomery
  H&L: Martha Logue; Mary Slade; Lovicy Deaver; Mary Deaver; Elizabeth Amos; Sarah McComas; James Montgomery; Mary Montgomery; Orpah Glenn.

WILLIAM WALLIS
  DOD: September 17, 1839    ADM: John Quarles
  H&L: Mary Wallis, widow; Henry Wallis; Richard Wallis; Jane Wallis; Eliza Wallis.

WILLIAM BAY
  DOD: December 31, 1839    ADM: John McFaddon
  H&L: Sarah Bay, widow; Arabella Bay; Kennedy Bay; Ann Bay; William Bay; Mary Bay.

JAMES B. HERBERT
  DOD: March 10, 1840    ADM: Mary Ann Smith
  H&L: Mary Ann Smith, widow; Margaret Rebecca Herbert, "the only child."

WILLIAM G. McCLURE
  DOD: March 17, 1840    ADM: Thomas Bay
  H&L: Martha McComas, widow; Asenath Ann Bay; Margaret Smith; German McComas; James McClure; Elizabeth McClure; John McClure; William McClure.

AMOS McCOMAS
  DOD: April 7, 1840    ADM: Isabella McComas
  H&L: Isabella McComas, widow; William McComas; James McComas; Nathan H. McComas; Ann McComas; Aquila McComas; Robert McComas; Isabella McComas; Amos McComas; John G. McComas.

FERDINAND G. BAGELY
  DOD: November 24, 1840    ADM: John O. Bagely
  H&L: Elizabeth Keys, sister; To Susan Ruth's heirs; To Mary Ruth's heirs; George W. Bagely; John O. Bagely; Samuel H. Bagely; William A. Bagely; Cunningham S. Ramsay, who married a sister of the deceased; To Lavenia R. Sappington's heirs.

WILLIAM MILES
  DOD: August 14, 1838    ADM: Aquila Miles
  H&L: J. W. Walker; Aquila Miles; William Miles; George P. Cook; Charles Whitelock; Mitchell J. Smith; James Lytle; Herman Stump; Joseph Hopkins; John Levy; Samuel Magan; William Stephenson, of George; James Stephenson; William Wilson.

DANIEL POCOCK
  DOD: December 22, 1840    ADM: William Hutchins
  H&L: Daniel Pocock; James Pocock; Elijah Pocock.

PETER KLINEFELTER
  DOD: March 3, 1840    ADM: John Klinefelter and John S. Norris
  H&L: Mary Klinefelter, widow; Mary Klinefelter; John Klinefelter; Mary Wadworth; Ann Hughes; Jesse Klinefelter.

JOSHUA BLANEY
  DOD: May 12, 1840    ADM: Mary St. Clair
  H&L: Thomas Blaney's heirs; Mary St. Clair, sister.

MAHLON H. WEST
    DOD: 1840                    ADM: Mary T. and William S. West
    H&L: Mary T. West, widow; William S. West, son; Jesse H. West, son;
         Rebecca T. Roman, daughter; Elizabeth H. West, daughter; Mary
         S. West, daughter; Granville T. West, son; Edward S. West, son.

THOMAS N. HENDERSON
    DOD: June 9, 1840             ADM: Archibald Henderson
    H&L: Jane N. Henderson, widow; Alice Ann Henderson, daughter;
         Sarah E. Henderson, daughter.

DAVID McCLASKEY
    DOD: June 15, 1841            ADM: Sally McClaskey
    H&L: Mary McClaskey; Sally McClaskey; Evelina McClaskey; Minerva
         McClaskey; Eleanora McClaskey; William H. McClaskey.

WILLIAM McNUTT
    DOD: June 16, 1840   ADM: Wakeman B. Hopkins & Samuel G. McNutt
    H&L: Olive McNutt, mother of the deceased; Rebecca McNutt, sister;
         John McNutt, brother; Samuel G. McNutt; Dr. W. B. Hopkins.

JOHN NORRIS
    DOD: June 16, 1840            ADM: Alexander Norris
    H&L: Alexander Norris; Sarah Norris; Elizabeth Norris; and, to
         negro Charles ($).

WILLIAM TUCKER
    DOD: July 28, 1840            ADM: Rebecca Tucker
    H&L: Rebecca Tucker, widow; William P. Tucker; Thomas H. Tucker.

AMOS CORD
    DOD: February 16, 1841        ADM: John H. Cord
    H&L: Catherine Cord, widow; Mary Cord; John H. Cord; Thomas Cord;
         Elizabeth Cord; Averilla J. Cord; Susanna Cord.

MARY B. WILLIS
    DOD: September 7, 1841        ADM: Edmund L. Bull
    H&L: Sarah Bull, mother of the deceased; Ann Bull, sister;
         Margaret Bull, sister; Rachel Bull, sister; John Bull,
         brother; Edmund L. Bull, brother; William L. Bull, brother,
         Bennet Bull, brother.

NATHANIEL HOSKINS
    DOD: September 21, 1841   ADM: David Preston & Cheyney Hoskins
    H&L: Jesse Hoskins, son; Edith Hoskins, daughter; Martha Jane
         Hollingsworth, daughter; Sarah Ann Hoskins, daughter;
         Phebe Hannah Hoskins, daughter.

THOMAS STREET
    DOD: November 2, 1841    ADM: John Street and Merryman Street
    H&L: John Street; Merryman Street; William Street; James
         Augustus Street; Thomas Street; Sarah Leatha Street;
         Martha Ann Street; Catherine Street, widow.

JESSE POTEET
    DOD: December 14, 1841        ADM: Martin Guyton
    H&L: Laura Poteet; Jesse Poteet.

REBECCA TUCKER
    DOD: December 14, 1841        ADM: James Paul

REBECCA TUCKER (continued)
 H&L: Thomas Tucker; William P. Tucker.

JOHN FORWOOD
 DOD: July 26, 1842    ADM: Parker Forwood
 H&L: Elizabeth Johnson; James W. Williams; T. A. Hays; N. Hays; Joseph Parker; Samuel Stump; Ducket Stump.

PARKER MITCHELL
 DOD: February 28, 1843    ADM: Jane Mitchell
 H&L: Jane Mitchell, widow; John Parker Mitchell, son; Frederick Neill Mitchell, son; George U. Mitchell, son; Charles W. Mitchell, son.

JOHN SINGLETON
 DOD: April 4, 1843    ADM: Amos Singleton
 H&L: Jacob Singleton; John Singleton; Sarah Ann Everett; Herman Singleton; Amos Singleton.

ABRAHAM J. THOMAS
 DOD: April 12, 1842    ADM: Joseph Coudon
 H&L: Elizabeth J. Richards; Herman S. Thomas; Eleanor L. Thomas; Oliver H. Thomas; Hannah S. Thomas; William T. Thomas.

 DOD: March 19, 1844    ADM and H&L: Same as April 12, 1842.

 DOD: May 6, 1845    ADM and H&L: Same as April 12, 1842.

WILLIAM CHESNEY
 DOD: May 23, 1843    ADM: William Chesney
 H&L: To Thomas Chesney's heirs; James C. Chesney; Ann Wood; Mary Quinby; Susan Everett; Benjamin Chesney; William Chesney; Jesse Chesney; John Chesney.

BENJAMIN SILLOCK
 DOD: October 11, 1842    ADM: Nathaniel Sillock
 H&L: Hannah Sillock, widow; Nathaniel Sillock; Honford Sillock; Benjamin Sillock.

JAMES AMOSS
 DOD: June 29, 1843    Distribution of Negroes to:
 Abraham Amoss; John T. Amoss; George R. Amoss; Catherine Hall, wife of Aquila Hall; Sarah Amoss; to heirs of Isaac Amoss, decd.

ELIZABETH CHAUNCEY
 DOD: November 22, 1843    Distribution of Negroes to:
 Susan Sutton; Mary Veazey; Benjamin Chauncey.

WILLIAM ADAMS
 DOD: April 9, 1844    ADM: John and William Adams
 H&L: Ely B. Adams; Caroline G. Adams; John Adams; William Adams; Hannah Hughes; Susan G. Adams.

MARY GORRELL
 DOD: May 21, 1844    ADM: John Dever
 H&L: Hannah Dever; Thomas Dever; Elizabeth Dever.

HESTER CARMAN
 DOD: June 11, 1844    ADM: Elijah and Caleb Carman
 H&L: Elijah Carman; Hester Kennedy; Nancy Chappel; Caleb Carman; Robert Carman.

DENNIS COCHLAN
  DOD: June 25, 1844          ADM: Samuel Smith
  H&L: To Rev. James Reed for erection of Catholic Church in
       Havre de Grace; Dennis Kaup; James Baxter; David Keefe;
       John Erwin; William Noyle.

WILLIAM MICHAEL
  DOD: August 6, 1844          ADM: James Walker
  H&L: Sarah Ann Michael; Hannah Michael; James W. Michael;
       George T. Michael.

JOHN MARTIN
  DOD: November 19, 1844        ADM: Daniel Martin
  H&L: Daniel Martin; Catherine Gallup; Henry Martin; Louisa
       Swift; John Martin; Eliza Martin; Louisa Martin; George
       Martin.

JAMES STEPHENSON
  DOD: November 22, 1844        ADM: William B. Stephenson
  H&L: William B. Stephenson; Robert Stephenson; and, William B.
       Stephenson in trust for Eliza, Ann, Susannah, Margaret and
       Hannah Stephenson.

ELIZABETH CHAUNCEY
  DOD: January 7, 1845          ADM: Samuel Sutton
  H&L: Susan Sutton; Mary Veazey; Benjamin Chauncey.

WILLIAM GLENN
  DOD: December 31, 1844        ADM: Robert and Nathan Glenn
  H&L: William Glenn; Temperance Clark; Rebecca Glenn, widow;
       Isabella McComas; Rebecca Ross.

AARON HARKINS
  DOD: 1845                     ADM: Joseph Harkins & David Tucker
  H&L: Sarah Harkins, widow; Stephen Harkins; William Harkins;
       Joseph Harkins; Jane Collins; Sarah Wilkinson; Rachel
       Tucker; Hannah Holland; John Harkins.

THOMAS H. ROBERTS
  DOD: April 1, 1845            ADM: Margaret Streett (Roberts)
  H&L: Margaret Streett, formerly Roberts, widow; John B. Roberts;
       William R. Roberts; George H. Roberts; Thomas H. Roberts.

HANNAH FULTON
  DOD: April 1, 1845            ADM: Benjamin S. Amoss
  H&L: To heirs of Ann Ditto, namely, William Ditto, Martha Wilson,
       and Mary Hitchcock; To heirs of Robert Amos, namely, Martha
       Rigdon, Sarah Gilbert, Benjamin Amos, Mary Ann Miller, James
       Amos, Corbin Amos, Elizabeth Logue, Ann Amos, Ellen Amos and
       Robert Amos; To heirs of Elizabeth Divers, namely, Annanias
       Divers, John Divers and Daniel Amos; To heirs of James Amoss,
       "names unknown;" Martha McComas; Joshua Amos; Corbin Amos;
       Benjamin S. Amos.

WILLIAM STEPHENSON
  DOD: April 18, 1845           ADM: Elizabeth Stephenson
  H&L: Hetty Stephenson, widow; Hetty Stephenson; Hannah Stephenson;
       To heirs of Mary Ann Stephenson; Sarah Parker; Elizabeth
       Stephenson.

HUGH SMITH
DOD: April 15, 1845  ADN: Christopher Wilson, Jr.
H&L: Martha Smith; Margaret Smith; Hugh Smith; John Smith; Margaret Smith, widow.

WILLIAM ADAMS
DOD: April 15, 1845  ADM: John and William Adams
H&L: Eli B. Adams; Caroline G. Adams; John Adams; William Adams; Hannah C. Hughes; Susan G. Adams.
DOD: September 9, 1845  ADM and H&L: Same as April 15, 1845.

JOHN FORWOOD
DOD: May 6, 1845  ADM: Parker Forwood
H&L: James Alexander; William Lindsay; Edward Bussey; Joseph Warner; James McLaughlin; Joseph Guyton; James Harvey; George Rider; John Preston; Joseph Parker; Samuel Stump; Elizabeth Johnson; T. A. Hays; N. Hays; Ducket Stump.

HUGH SMITH
DOD: April 15, 1845  ADN: Christopher Wilson, Jr.
H&L: Thomas Smith; Rachel Wilson; William Smith; Hannah Huff; Elizabeth Holloway; Hetty Wilson; Mary Bagely; Reubin Smith; Martha Duncan.

WILLIAM CLARK
DOD: June 10, 1845  ADM: Barnet J. Clark & Thomas Clark
H&L: Ruth Quinlan; Barnet J. Clark; Thomas Clark; William Clark.

CALEB PUE
DOD: June 10, 1845  ADM: Michael E. Pue
H&L: Elizabeth Pue, widow; Michael E. Pue; Mary E. Kennard; Rebecca Pue.

JAMES AMOSS
DOD: July 29, 1845  ADM: George R. Amoss
H&L: John T. Amoss, brother; Abraham Amoss, brother; George R. Amoss, brother; Catherine Hall, sister; Sarah Amoss, sister; To heirs of Isaac Amos, deceased, namely, William W. Amos, Catherine A. Plasket, Sarah E. Raymond, James W. Amoss, and Margaret H. Myers.

JESSE TAYLOR
DOD: February 7, 1846  ADM: Cooper L. Boyd
H&L: Sarah McColly, daughter; Frances Crawford, daughter; Milcha Boyd, daughter.

THOMAS SCOTT
DOD: February 24, 1846  ADM: Henry D. Bowyer
H&L: Ross Scott, son; Ann J. Bowyer, daughter.

CATHERINE YORK
DOD: March 31, 1846  ADM: John E. McComas
H&L: Elizabeth Wilson; Angelina Wilson; William Waltham; Catherine Waltham; James Carta; Ann Carta; John Carta.

ESTATE DISTRIBUTION OF JOHN HALL, HARFORD COUNTY, MARYLAND, 1802

Dr. Josias Hall Administrator Debonis Non of John Hall of Cranbury Deceased

| | | £ s d |
|---|---|---|
| To Ballance of your final account | | 1577 18 5 |
| Deduct for Widows thirds and Legacies to Edward Hall John B. Hall & Josias Hall — — — — £650..9..5¼ | | |
| Ballance for distribution among the following persons by the deceased Will (To wit) Avarilla, Priscilla, Mary and Elizabeth | | 927 8 11 |

By Distribution and Legacies as follows (to wit)
By the widows thirds £ 525..19..5¼
By Legacies willed the Edwd Hall to wit
Negro Sharper appraised to £80, one Silver Watch appraised to £3, one Silver hilted Cuttlass £2..10..0, one pair Silver Hilted Pistols £2..10..0 amounting to — 87..10..0
By Legacies willed the John B Hall to wit, one Small Sword and Tobacco Box appraised to 2..0..0
By Do. willed the Josias Hall to wit, one horse called Rover £17..10..0, one Saddle & Bridle $3, one negro boy named Hercules a Gift allowed by the Court £15 amounting to — 35..10..0
£ 650..9..5¼

| | £ s d |
|---|---|
| By Avarilla Patterson | 231 17 2¾ |
| By Priscilla Christie | 231 17 2¾ |
| By Mary Hall | 231 17 2¾ |
| By Elizabeth Hall | 231 17 2¾ |
| | 927 8 11 |

March the 22d 1802 This account Examined and passed by the Court
Wm Jarrett RW7C ly
ey by AS

## SURNAME INDEX

Adams 49, 51
Albert 20
Alderson 24
Aldridge 28
Alexander 18
Allen 28, 34, 39, 42, 43
Allender 8, 22
Amos (Amoss) 20, 22, 23, 24,
    36, 41, 46, 47, 49, 50, 51
Anderson 1, 2, 12, 32, 37
Archer 10, 21, 39, 44, 45
Armstrong 1, 4, 13
Arnold 37
Ashinhorst 9
Asbury 28
Ashton 45
Ayres 5, 18

Bagely 47, 51
Bailey 41
Baker 4, 5, 13, 14
Balderson 2, 5, 7
Baldwin 29, 34
Bankhead 39
Bare 12, 17
Barling 32
Barnes 7, 14, 17, 24, 30, 35
Barnett 14
Barrett 4
Barron 40, 42
Bateman 31, 33
Baust 20
Baxter 10, 35, 50
Bay 47
Bayless 6, 11, 16, 35
Beans 4
Beard 21
Beaty (Beatty) 4, 29, 33, 39, 43
Bell 20
Benson 19, 25
Bevard 21
Biddison 1
Biddle 18
Billingslea (Billingsley) 14, 32, 46
Binns 1
Birckhead 11, 24, 31, 33, 43
Blackburn 44
Blaney 19, 22, 36, 47
Boarman 17
Bolton 31
Bolster 27, 32
Boman 1, 6
Bonar (Boner) 4, 5
Bond 4, 17, 24, 27, 33, 34, 40
Bosley 41

Botts 10, 16, 45
Bowyer 51
Bowzer 21
Boyd 39, 51
Bradley 9
Bradford 27, 44, 45
Brannen 27
Branson 15, 19
Brewer 34
Brinley 1
Brinton 17
Brooks 19
Brown 4, 5, 6, 11, 16, 23, 31,
    42, 44
Browning 5
Brownley 5, 16, 18, 27, 34
Bryarly (Bryerly, Briarly) 3,
    6, 9, 14, 20, 33, 38
Buckingham 44
Bull 2, 12, 13, 15, 27, 29, 32,
    39, 48
Burnett 2
Bussey 4, 25, 51
Butler 18, 45

Cain 2, 40
Calder 11
Calvert 34
Calwell 29, 31
Campbell 9, 21
Canady 22
Cannon 17, 20, 32, 43, 45
Car 24
Careins 28, 29, 31, 35
Carlin 37
Carman 13, 37, 43, 49
Carta 51
Carter 12
Carver (Caver) 26
Cato 44, 46
Chain 32
Chambers 23
Chapman 7
Chappell (Chappel) 43, 49
Chauncey (Chancey) 4, 21, 25,
    27, 33, 38, 42, 49, 50
Chelson 3
Chesney 31, 32, 49
Chew 26, 33, 34, 38
Chisholm 44
Chocke 39
Christie 1, 36, 52
Clark 2, 17, 34, 45, 50, 51
Clendenin (Clendinen) 25, 33, 42
Cochlan 50

Cochran 13
Cole (Coale)  8, 9, 10, 16, 22,
    36, 37, 39, 46
Collins  50
Collis  26
Connally (Connolly)  8, 24
Cook  47
Cooper  4, 5, 6, 32
Corbet  6
Cord  3, 48
Coudon (Condon)  40, 49
Courtney  8, 10, 21, 22, 24, 37, 46
Covington  14
Cowen (Cowan)  5, 9, 21, 22, 25, 27
Cox  8, 11, 16
Crawford  1, 31, 39
Criswell  4, 23, 24, 38
Crockett  6
Crossmore  10
Cunningham  28, 40, 41
Curry  21
Curtin  9

Dallam  9, 10, 11, 23, 42
Davis  5, 13, 33, 37, 39, 46
Dawes  16, 25
Day  2, 4, 26, 28
Deaver (Dever)  13, 19, 20, 21, 27, 49
Debrular (Debruler)  7, 29
Deleporte  33
Demoss (Demos)  29, 39, 43, 44
Denbow  10, 35
Dillon  41
Disney  1
Ditto  50
Diven  13
Divers  50
Dods  6
Donagan (Dunnagan)  6, 17
Donn  46
Donovan (Donnovan)  21, 22
Dorney  33
Dorsey  5, 13, 20, 41
Douelle  46
Dougherty  2
Dove  21, 38, 44, 46
Drew  9
Dulaney (Dulany)  15, 20, 41
Duncan  25, 51
Dunn  21, 22
Durbin  45
Durham  4, 10, 11
Dutton  2, 7
Dyer  24

Eckhooff  18
Ecoff  25, 30, 38
Elliott  40

Ellis  16, 29, 30
Ely  2, 5, 7, 31
Enlows  38, 39
Erwin  50
Evans  20
Everist (Everst)  4, 8, 15, 23,
    29, 31
Everitt (Everett)  21, 46, 49
Evott  4, 5

Falls  11
Fareall  44
Fickey  40
Finney (Finny)  14
Ford (Foard)  3, 4, 10, 18, 22,
    23, 27
Forwood  15, 19, 34, 40, 43,
    49, 51
Foster  22
Fowler  3
Fuller  35
Fullerton  21, 22
Fulton  12, 17, 34, 44, 50
Fye (Fie)  3

Gallion  9, 23, 36, 46
Gallup  13, 42, 45
Games  7
Garrett  7
Garrettson  5, 12, 44
Garrison  22, 26, 28
Ghenn  25
Gibson  6, 18
Gilbert  12, 14, 15, 18, 24,
    26, 27, 32, 41, 50
Giles  45
Gilpin  41
Gittings  37, 39
Gladden  40, 41
Glascow  3
Glasgow  33, 35
Glenn  4, 7, 47, 50
Golsmith  4
Gorden  8
Gorrell  4, 20, 49
Gorsuch  7, 45
Gover  11, 13, 16, 19, 25
Grafton  24, 28, 30
Grant  34
Graves  9, 13
Green  4, 6, 17, 24, 35
Greenfield  8, 13
Greenland  16
Greer  15
Greme  9, 10
Griffith  5
Grindall  25
Groves  8

Guyton  23, 29, 31, 39, 40, 43, 48

Haden  40
Haflin  40
Halbfus  17
Hall  1, 13, 18, 19, 29, 34, 36,
    46, 49, 51, 52
Hammitt  22
Hanley  8
Hanna (Hana)  25, 30, 33, 34, 44
Hanson  3, 13, 21, 22, 26, 46
Harkins  50
Harkins  18
Harlon  41
Harris  11, 26
Harryman  39
Harvey  34, 43, 51
Haslep  31
Hatton  40
Haughey  40
Hawkins  12, 16, 23, 24, 34, 36
Hays  4, 10, 11, 19, 32, 39, 49,
    51
Heaton  3
Hellen  11
Henly  3
Henderson  24, 26, 27, 38, 48
Hendon  37
Herbert  37, 47
Hicks  27
Hill  13, 29, 36
Hillen  4, 11
Hillis  38
Hipkins  43
Hitchcock  27, 50
Holland  21, 50
Hollingsworth  48
Hollis  13, 20, 32
Holloway  51
Hoofman  21
Hooper  13
Hope  1, 28, 29, 32, 38
Hopkins  1, 11, 18, 26, 27, 33,
    34, 45, 47, 48
Horner  1
Hoskins  48
How  20
Howard  3
Hudson  36
Huff  51
Hughes (Hughs)  1, 8, 9, 10, 11,
    16, 17, 18, 22, 28, 29, 31,
    39, 43, 47, 49, 51
Hughston  2, 7, 8
Hugo  41
Husband  44
Huskins  10, 13
Huston  38
Hutchins  47

Ingram (Ingrim)  4, 20
Inlows  9
Irvin  38

Jackson  37
James  3, 19
Jarrett  8, 14, 26, 27, 39
Jarvis  40, 42, 43
Jay  23
Jeffery (Jeffrey)  6, 14, 17, 40
Jenkins  13, 14
Jenny  8
Jervis  43
Jibb  18
Jolly  10
Johns  2, 16
Johnson  9, 11, 15, 16, 23,
    40, 42, 45, 49, 51
Jones  1, 11, 44
Jordan  42

Kain  41
Kane  42
Kaup  50
Keefe  50
Keenan  40
Kelsey  24
Kelso  35
Kenly  1, 6, 33
Kennard  45, 51
Kennedy  22, 43, 49
Kentlemyers  24
Keys  47
Kidd  14
Kimberley  15
Kimble  5, 8, 9
Kirkwood  15, 29, 37
Klinefelter  47
Knight  27

Lammott  21
Lancaster  12, 21, 22, 23
Lansdale  43, 45, 46
Lawhead  8
Lawson  19
Lee  3, 13, 17, 19, 25, 30,
    32, 39, 46
Lemmon  46
Leonard  8
Lester  20
Levy  24, 35, 47
Lilly (Lilley)  6, 17, 40
Lindsay (Lindsey)  3, 6, 51
Litton  3
Livingston  20, 21
Loflin  37
Logan  35

Logue  6, 47, 50
Loney  34
Lowry  14, 34
Lukens  10, 11
Lynch  19
Lytle  47

Magan  47
Magness  10, 34
Mahan  28
Mahone  35
Mallet  28
Mannahan (Manahan)  25, 30
Marchand  33
Martain  5, 12, 14
Martin  14, 30, 46, 50
Massey  8
Matson  8
Matthews (Mathews)  7, 26, 27, 34, 37, 39
Maulsby (Malsby)  19, 27
McCally  39
McCandless  10, 19, 23
McCausling  3
McClaskey  16, 48
McClure  36, 37, 47
McComas  18, 19, 32, 36, 46, 47, 50, 51
McConkey  16
McCracken  4, 20
McCubbin  39
McElhiney  43
McElrath  4
McFaddon (McFadden)  22, 34, 47
McFall  9
McGaw  37, 38, 44
McGay  20
McGovern  10, 13
McGraw  15
McKendre  28
McKennon  33
McKernan  7
McLaughlin  19, 40, 51
McMasters  22, 26
McMath  6, 42
McNabb  10
McNutt  48
McWilliams  3
Meads  17, 29, 39, 43
Michael  1, 8, 13, 20, 21, 22, 23, 44, 50
Middleditch  18
Miles  7, 17, 22, 26, 47
Miller  23, 31, 34, 39, 44, 46, 50
Miscimmons  28
Mitchell  1, 3, 9, 12, 17, 18, 27, 31, 37, 40, 44, 46, 49
Monks  3

Montgomery  38, 47
Moore (Moor)  19, 22
Moores  3, 13, 25, 33, 38, 46
Morford  12
Morgan  26, 32, 33, 34, 40, 41
Morris  30
Murphy (MUrphey)  1, 2
Murry  12, 17
Myers (Myres)  8, 35, 51


Nelson  21, 22, 28, 29, 30, 33, 36
Norris  4, 7, 9, 12, 13, 25, 28, 32, 35, 36, 47, 48
Noyle  50


O'Brian (O'Brien)  10, 11, 18, 28, 31, 40, 46
O'Conor  19
O'Daniel  13
Offley  8
O'Neal  18
O'Neill  46
Onion  28, 41, 43
Osborn  1, 8, 13, 20, 21, 22, 29, 44

Pannell  40
Parker  41, 43, 49, 50, 51
Parsons  12, 24
Patterson  1, 3, 28, 40, 52
Paul  46, 48
Payne  36
Perdue  3
Perine (Prine)  13, 14
Perry  4
Perryman  26
Pitcock  7, 26, 45
Plasket  51
Pocock  47
Pogue  16
Pool  14
Porter  38
Poteet  3, 25, 42, 48
Powell (Powel)  9, 13
Presbury  5, 13, 19, 25, 45
Preston  3, 10, 19, 43, 48, 51
Price  20, 37, 41, 43, 45
Prigg  15, 16, 42
Pritchard  37
Pue  51
Pusey  16
Pyle  3, 16, 17, 18, 25, 35, 44


Quarles  47
Quinby  49
Quinlan  15, 25, 38, 51

Ralston (Rolston)  22, 26
Rampley  29, 39, 43
Ramsey (Ramsay)  16, 33, 34, 47
Ray  14, 17
Raymond  51
Rearden  31, 33
Reed  27, 50
Rees  3
Reese  30
Renshaw  2, 15, 17
Richards  49
Richardson  4, 19, 34
Richey (Richie)  14, 17
Ricketts  34, 35
Rider  43, 51
Rigbie  2
Rigdon  6, 8, 19, 30, 50
Ritaker  42
Riston  17
Roberts  7, 30, 46, 50
Robinson  11, 18
Rodgers  25, 36
Rogers  31, 44
Roman  48
Ross  50
Rouse  41, 43
Ruff  22, 23, 24, 27
Rumsay  37, 39
Ruth  47
Rutledge  24, 28, 32
Rutter  43

St. Clair  1, 13, 19, 30, 31, 35, 42, 47
Sanders  4
Sappington  35, 47
Saunders  44
Scarff (Scarf)  7, 14, 28
Scott  44, 51
Seth  8
Shaw  26
Shay  15
Sheredine (Sheridine)  1, 4
Shekell (Sheckell)  21, 32, 43
Sidwell  44
Sillock  41, 42, 49
Silvers  16
Simmons  23
Sims  20
Singleton  49
Skinner  27
Slade  31, 33, 35, 47
Smith  4, 5, 6, 12, 18, 19, 20, 23, 24, 25, 30, 31, 37, 38, 39, 40, 42, 45, 46, 47, 50, 51
Smithson  13, 19, 25, 30
Spence  27
Spencer  2, 12, 21, 23, 30, 31

Stallings  31
Stallion  30
Stallions  9
Standiford  37, 40
Stephens  43
Stephenson  6, 8, 14, 16, 45, 47, 50
Stewart  13
Stiles  9
Stockton  28
Stokes  28, 34
Streett (Street)  7, 28, 36, 40, 41, 45, 48, 50
Stroble  5
Strong  11
Stroud  9, 11
Stump  5, 8, 14, 20, 31, 39, 43, 44, 45, 47, 49, 51
Summers  4
Sutherland  36
Sutton  49, 50
Swift  46, 50

Tarbert  33
Tate  18
Taylor  2, 4, 5, 8, 10, 13, 15, 21, 39, 43, 45, 51
Terrell  36
Thomas  3, 6, 17, 18, 25, 30, 37, 38, 49
Thompson  14, 21, 22, 24, 25, 40
Thomson  35
Timmons  45
Tindley  13
Toland  35
Tonyhill  31
Townsend  25
Townsley  5, 11, 18
Tredway  17, 34, 35, 37, 39, 43, 44
Trimble  41
Trott  31
Troutner  36
Trulock  27
Tucker  32, 38, 45, 48, 49, 50
Turner  36

Valient  42
Vance  15
Vanclave  3
Vandegrift  17, 24
Vanhorn  21
Vansickle  21, 25, 27, 29, 30, 38
Varnal  27
Veazey  35, 49, 50
Vernay  18, 20

Wadsworth  36
Wadworth  47
Walker  47, 50

Wallis  8, 9, 47
Walter  36
Waltham (Walthom)  44, 51
Ward  1, 3, 9, 11, 12, 14, 30, 37
Wareham  28
Warfield  8
Warner  2, 5, 25, 45, 51
Watkins  26
Watson  31, 32
Watt  36, 37, 40, 41
Watters  4, 11, 12, 13, 22, 23, 26,
    27, 34, 38, 39, 44
Way  10, 24
Wayminn  24
Weatherall (Wetherall)  2, 4, 24, 31, 33
Webster  17, 20, 21, 27, 28
Weeks  32, 33
Welch  13, 19
Wesley  6, 45
West  10, 13, 28, 38, 48
Wheeler  6, 17, 25, 31, 42
Whitaker  6, 31, 35
White  9
Whiteford  6, 33
Whitelock  47
Whiten  8
Whitson  23, 24
Wiley  4, 5, 25
Wilkinson  50
Williams  14, 25, 40, 41, 44, 49
Willis  48
Wilmer  39
Wilson  3, 8, 12, 15, 23, 27, 30, 31,
    33, 35, 37, 41, 45, 46, 47, 50, 51
Wood  35, 46, 49
Woodard  7
Woodward  26
Woolen  26
Worsley  6
Worthington  3, 9, 33, 38


Yearly  19
York  29, 51
Young  11, 19, 45

Other books by the author:

*A Closer Look at St. John's Parish Registers [Baltimore County, Maryland], 1701-1801*
*A Collection of Maryland Church Records*
*A Guide to Genealogical Research in Maryland: 5th Edition, Revised and Enlarged*
*Abstracts of the Ledgers and Accounts of the Bush Store and Rock Run Store, 1759-1771*
*Abstracts of the Orphans Court Proceedings of Harford County, 1778-1800*
*Abstracts of Wills, Harford County, Maryland, 1800-1805*
*Baltimore City [Maryland] Deaths and Burials, 1834-1840*
*Baltimore County, Maryland, Overseers of Roads, 1693-1793*
*Bastardy Cases in Baltimore County, Maryland, 1673-1783*
*Bastardy Cases in Harford County, Maryland, 1774-1844*
*Bible and Family Records of Harford County, Maryland Families: Volume V*
*Children of Harford County: Indentures and Guardianships, 1801-1830*
*Colonial Delaware Soldiers and Sailors, 1638-1776*
*Colonial Families of the Eastern Shore of Maryland
Volumes 5, 6, 7, 8, 9, 11, 12, 13, 14, and 16*
*Colonial Maryland Soldiers and Sailors, 1634-1734*
*Dr. John Archer's First Medical Ledger, 1767-1769, Annotated Abstracts*
*Early Anglican Records of Cecil County*
*Early Harford Countians, Individuals Living in Harford County, Maryland in Its Formative Years
Volume 1: A to K, Volume 2: L to Z, and Volume 3: Supplement*
*Harford County Taxpayers in 1870, 1872 and 1883*
*Harford County, Maryland Divorce Cases, 1827-1912: An Annotated Index*
*Heirs and Legatees of Harford County, Maryland, 1774-1802*
*Heirs and Legatees of Harford County, Maryland, 1802-1846*
*Inhabitants of Baltimore County, Maryland, 1763-1774*
*Inhabitants of Cecil County, Maryland, 1649-1774*
*Inhabitants of Harford County, Maryland, 1791-1800*
*Inhabitants of Kent County, Maryland, 1637-1787*
*Joseph A. Pennington & Co., Havre De Grace, Maryland Funeral Home Records:
Volume II, 1877-1882, 1893-1900*
*Maryland Bible Records, Volume 1: Baltimore and Harford Counties*
*Maryland Bible Records, Volume 2: Baltimore and Harford Counties*
*Maryland Bible Records, Volume 3: Carroll County*
*Maryland Bible Records, Volume 4: Eastern Shore*
*Maryland Deponents, 1634-1799*
*Maryland Deponents: Volume 3, 1634-1776*
*Maryland Public Service Records, 1775-1783: A Compendium of Men and Women of
Maryland Who Rendered Aid in Support of the American Cause against
Great Britain during the Revolutionary War*
*Marylanders to Carolina: Migration of Marylanders to
North Carolina and South Carolina prior to 1800*

*Marylanders to Kentucky, 1775-1825*

*Methodist Records of Baltimore City, Maryland: Volume 1, 1799-1829*

*Methodist Records of Baltimore City, Maryland: Volume 2, 1830-1839*

*Methodist Records of Baltimore City, Maryland: Volume 3, 1840-1850 (East City Station)*

*More Maryland Deponents, 1716-1799*

*More Marylanders to Carolina: Migration of Marylanders to North Carolina and South Carolina prior to 1800*

*More Marylanders to Kentucky, 1778-1828*

*Outpensioners of Harford County, Maryland, 1856-1896*

*Presbyterian Records of Baltimore City, Maryland, 1765-1840*

*Quaker Records of Baltimore and Harford Counties, Maryland, 1801-1825*

*Quaker Records of Northern Maryland, 1716-1800*

*Quaker Records of Southern Maryland, 1658-1800*

*Revolutionary Patriots of Anne Arundel County, Maryland*

*Revolutionary Patriots of Baltimore Town and Baltimore County, 1775-1783*

*Revolutionary Patriots of Calvert and St. Mary's Counties, Maryland, 1775-1783*

*Revolutionary Patriots of Caroline County, Maryland, 1775-1783*

*Revolutionary Patriots of Cecil County, Maryland*

*Revolutionary Patriots of Charles County, Maryland, 1775-1783*

*Revolutionary Patriots of Delaware, 1775-1783*

*Revolutionary Patriots of Dorchester County, Maryland, 1775-1783*

*Revolutionary Patriots of Frederick County, Maryland, 1775-1783*

*Revolutionary Patriots of Harford County, Maryland, 1775-1783*

*Revolutionary Patriots of Kent and Queen Anne's Counties*

*Revolutionary Patriots of Lancaster County, Pennsylvania*

*Revolutionary Patriots of Maryland, 1775-1783: A Supplement*

*Revolutionary Patriots of Maryland, 1775-1783: Second Supplement*

*Revolutionary Patriots of Montgomery County, Maryland, 1776-1783*

*Revolutionary Patriots of Prince George's County, Maryland, 1775-1783*

*Revolutionary Patriots of Talbot County, Maryland, 1775-1783*

*Revolutionary Patriots of Worcester and Somerset Counties, Maryland, 1775-1783*

*Revolutionary Patriots of Washington County, Maryland, 1776-1783*

*St. George's (Old Spesutia) Parish, Harford County, Maryland: Church and Cemetery Records, 1820-1920*

*St. John's and St. George's Parish Registers, 1696-1851*

*Survey Field Book of David and William Clark in Harford County, Maryland, 1770-1812*

*The Crenshaws of Kentucky, 1800-1995*

*The Delaware Militia in the War of 1812*

*Union Chapel United Methodist Church Cemetery Tombstone Inscriptions, Wilna, Harford County, Maryland*

www.ingramcontent.com/pod-product-compliance
Lightning Source LLC
Chambersburg PA
CBHW061511040426
42450CB00008B/1565